FRENCH LIBERALISM
1789-1848

MAJOR ISSUES IN HISTORY

Editor

C. WARREN HOLLISTER

University of California, Santa Barbara

FRENCH LIBERALISM
1789-1848

EDITED BY

Walter Simon

University of Keele,
Staffordshire, England

John Wiley & Sons, Inc.
New York • London • Sydney • Toronto

Library of Congress Catalogue Card Number: 71-178151

ISBN 0-471-79190-3

Printed in the United States of America.

10 9 8 7 6 5 4 3 2 1

Editor's Prepatory Note

The editorial matter in this volume is necessarily brief and therefore very general, "introductory" in the fullest sense of being intended to make the selections accessible. The selections themselves, by contrast, often contain detailed, subtle, and sophisticated arguments. Students are urged to read them with close attention in order to get the best out of them. They are also advised to be on the lookout for unstated assumptions, which can be as significant as explicit arguments.

W.M.S.

SERIES PREFACE

The reading program in a history survey course traditionally has consisted of a large two-volume textbook and, perhaps, a book of readings. This simple reading program requires few decisions and little imagination on the instructor's part, and tends to encourage in the student the virtue of careful memorization. Such programs are by no means things of the past, but they certainly do not represent the wave of the future.

The reading program in survey courses at many colleges and universities today is far more complex. At the risk of oversimplification, and allowing for many exceptions and overlaps, it can be divided into four categories: (1) textbook, (2) original source readings, (3) specialized historical essays and interpretive studies, and (4) historical problems.

After obtaining an overview of the course subject matter (textbook), sampling the original sources, and being exposed to selective examples of excellent modern historical writing (historical essays), the student can turn to the crucial task of weighing various possible interpretations of major historical issues. It is at this point that memory gives way to creative critical thought. The "problems approach," in other words, is the intellectual climax of a thoughtfully conceived reading program and is, indeed, the most characteristic of all approaches to historical pedagogy among the newer generation of college and university teachers.

The historical problems books currently available are many and varied. Why add to this information explosion? Because the Wiley Major Issues Series constitutes an endeavor to produce something new that will respond to pedagogical needs thus far unmet. First, it is a series of individual volumes—one per problem. Many good teachers would much prefer to select their own historical issues rather than be tied to an inflexible sequence of issues imposed by a publisher and bound together between two covers. Second, the Wiley Major Issues Series is based on the idea of approaching the significant problems of history through a deft interweaving of primary sources and secondary analysis, fused together by the skill of a scholar-editor. It is felt that the essence of a historical issue cannot be satisfactorily probed either by placing a body of undigested source materials into the hands of inexperienced students or by limiting these students to the controversial literature of modern scholars who debate the meaning of sources the student never sees. This series approaches historical problems by exposing students to both the finest historical thinking on the issue and some of the evidence on which this thinking is based. This synthetic approach should prove far more fruitful than either the raw-source approach or the exclusively second-hand approach, for it combines the advantages—and avoids the serious disadvantage—of both.

Finally, the editors of the individual volumes in the Major Issues Series have been chosen from among the ablest scholars in their fields. Rather than faceless referees, they are historians who know their issues from the inside and, in most instances, have themselves contributed significantly to the relevant scholarly literature. It has been the editorial policy of this series to permit the editor-scholars of the individual volumes the widest possible latitude both in formulating their topics and in organizing their materials. Their scholarly competence has been unquestioningly respected; they have been encouraged to approach the problems as they see fit. The titles and themes of the series volumes have been suggested in nearly every case by the scholar-editors themselves. The criteria have been (1) that the issue be of relevance to undergraduate lecture courses in history, and (2) that it be an issue which the scholar-editor knows thoroughly and in which he has done creative work. And, in general, the second criterion has been given precedence over the first. In short, the question "What are the significant historical issues today?" has been answered not by general editors or sales departments but by the scholar-teachers who are responsible for these volumes.

University of California,   *C. Warren Hollister*
Santa Barbara

CONTENTS

Contents

FRENCH LIBERALISM
1789-1848

INTRODUCTION

The word "liberal" in a political sense made its appearance in Spain in the early nineteenth century when it was applied to the small group of men plotting to oust the despotic king placed on the throne by the military force of his brother Napoleon Bonaparte and to secure "liberty" by installing in his place a regime limited by a fundamental law or constitution. The word and its derivations soon spread across Europe to describe similar ideas, movements, institutions, and people elsewhere. Like many other words—notably, for example, "humanist"—it has taken on a new meaning in the twentieth century and probably never meant quite the same in America in the first place, but it is with the original article, as applied to France, that this book is concerned. Not that the meeting is simple or unequivoval—on the contrary, it had many different shades and changed its emphasis even during the relatively short but very eventful period here involved. Indeed, were this not the case there would be little need for a book such as this at all: one or two examples of a standard brand of liberalism would suffice. But it is in fact one of the main purposes of the book to illustrate some of the very many facets that liberalism exhibited, and it must be one of the main functions of this introduction at least to suggest—space will allow for no more—some of the reasons for the variety.

Again like many other words, "liberal" and "liberalism" have been applied retrospectively to periods before the words existed, particularly by historians in search of the origins of the phenomenon they describe. This is an activity which can easily be overdone, and for our purposes, certainly, it is not necessary to go back farther than the end of the seventeenth century, to the political theory of John Locke and the Glorious Revolution of 1688 which vindicated limited constitutional monarchy based on

Natural Law against absolute or semiabsolute monarchy, whether also based on Natural Law as in Hobbes, on tradition as in Locke's other great antagonist Filmer, or on divine right as practised and defended in the France of Louis XIV.

In France itself it is usually the Baron de Montesquieu (1689-1755) who is regarded as the founder or at any rate the principal forerunner of liberalism. Montesquieu was much impressed not only by Locke but by the British constitution in practice as he understood it; in his turn Montesquieu was not only a principal influence on the authors of the *Federalist* papers and hence on the United States Constitution but also much discussed and debated by many of the French liberals of our period to whom he transmitted much of his Anglophilia. Although, like Locke, he believed in Natural Law only in a somewhat attenuated form, this was one of the grounds of debate; another was that Montesquieu defended "checks and balances" and the separation of powers (as they are found in the U.S. Constitution) not only on principle but—at least so it could be argued—as an aristocrat and a member of the French judiciary who because of his position had a vested interest in limiting the executive, that is, the monarchy of Louis XV. As such, so the argument runs, Montesquieu provided theoretical foundations for the "aristocratic resurgence" that manifested itself shortly after his death, that is to say for a reactionary social and political movement rather than for a "progressive" policy such as many liberals of our period prided themselves on pursuing.

This account indicates not only the potential ambiguity of liberalism in relation to doctrines to which it might be opposed but also the reduced relev*ance of problems and institutions characteristic of the ancien regime* once the Revolution had broken out. The men who gained control of France, the leaders of the National (later Constituent) Assembly, in the summer of 1789 can properly be classed as liberals: although their backgrounds, motivations, detailed ideas, and ultimate fates were different (two of them, Mounier and Mallet du Pan, are represented in the selections which follow, and another, Condorcet, should be counted with them though he was not a member of the National Assembly), they shared the basic premise that the monarchy should be preserved as an active political force but should be limited in scope by a constitution giving defined powers to an elected representative assembly. The most prominent achievements of these men while in power included the Declaration of the Rights of Man, the constitution of 1791, and the Le Chapelier law prohibiting workers' associations. But the period of their dominance was short; although one of their number above all, the Comte de Mirabeau (1749-1791), fought for their ideas until his death, the mistakes of Louis XVI and his queen, Marie Antoinette, combined with mounting pressure from an increasingly radical Paris populace placed the monarchy in increasing jeopardy. The leadership of the Revolution passed decisively into more radical and specifically republican hands by 1792, and the "liberals" of the preceding phase are accordingly often called the Moderates, especially in view of the Terror of the years 1793 to 1794 presided over by the radical Jacobins.

These were years of obscurity or exile, if not death, for men of liberal convictions. When, after Thermidor and the interlude of the Directory, Napoleon Bonaparte assumed power, first as Consul and later as Emperor, liberalism turned out to be in not much better case. Its foremost exponents during this period were a group of men who called themselves "Ideologues." Though also descended intellectually from Locke they were primarily interested in his epistemology as adapted by the French philosopher Etienne Bonnot de Condillac (1715-1780) who had emphasized the role of sensations, at the expense of reflection, more than Locke had done. The Ideologues, including P.J.G. Cabanis (1757-1808) as well as Destutt de Tracy and Daunou who are represented in this volume, were concerned with the mechanics of the mind and of language as the key to the formation of "ideas" and rejected all a priori systems. Politically this meant a rejection of any metaphysical concept of liberty and led instead to a utilitarian approach to the individual's place in society. Destutt de Tracy's disagreements with Montesquieu are based partly on an implicit agreement with Rousseau, the archenemy for the earlier generation of liberals such as Mounier, that "checks and balances" are unnecessary in a situation where the people can attain their own happiness as they see fit; but Tracy and especially Daunou are emphatic that such a situation requires guarantees of the individual's liberty.

Such sentiments were unwelcome to Napoleon; moreover he misunderstood the label "Ideologues," mistakenly applying it to idealists in the sense of utopians. Therefore he silenced them, and

Tracy's main political work was first published in English in Philadelphia. In return, Tracy was in the forefront of those responsible for Napoleon's fall in 1814. When the latter returned from Elba in 1815 for the Hundred Days he tried to learn from experience and govern in a more liberal spirit by means of an "Additional Act," a series of amendments to his previous constitution. This abortive act was largely the work of Benjamin Constant, a young writer with strong liberal convictions partly acquired from his mistress Mme. de Stael, who had spent most of Napoleon's reign abroad imbibing, in particular, the literary and nationalist liberalism of Germany which she tried to convey to the French. Between the two of them this pair produced the most closely reasoned case—reflecting in part the strong influence on them of the Enlightenment, which did not, of course, simply come to a halt in 1789—for the alliance of political and literary liberalism during the Bourbon Restoration of 1830.

This regime was based on the famous Charter issued by Louis XVIII in 1814 (with which Napoleon's Additional Act was intended to compete). The Charter was significant for its very existence, even disregarding its provisions: it represented the first formal constitution by which a Bourbon monarch had ever agreed to be bound. As such it did indeed, in the strict sense, introduce that constitutional monarchy which Mounier and Mirabeau had striven in vain to establish. But the restraints that were in fact placed on the monarchy were limited in scope; above all, sovereignty was vested clearly and solely in the monarchy, ministers being appointed by and responsible to him and not to the legislature which was elected on a very narrow property franchise. Not less important in view of the anticlericalism of the revolutionary tradition, the Charter reestablished the Roman Catholic Church as the state religion, with the result that the state was the dominant partner in the "Alliance between Throne and Altar," a condition deplored by Lamennais. Nevertheless the Charter appeared to many men of moderate or liberal principles to offer, if not an ideal, at least an acceptable political as well as religious compromise, a "happy medium" or *juste milieu,* between the *ancien regime* on the one hand and radical democracy on the other. This was the viewpoint characteristic of a group misleadingly called the Doctrinaires, among whom Cousin and Guizot were prominent. They were, however, before long both personally and politically disappointed with the regime in practice and joined such men as Constant in opposition to its increasingly reactionary character, especially after the accession of Charles X in 1824. Cousin, in particular, launched a liberal crusade which created the atmosphere conducive to the ultimate end of the Bourbon monarchy in the Revolution of 1830.

Both Cousin and Guizot played active political roles under the succeeding "July Monarchy." Guizot rose to serve Louis Philippe for many years as prime minister and, ironically, was in office when the July Monarchy was in turn overthrown in 1848. Guizot himself, in the two selections included, offers perhaps as good an account as any of this apparently paradoxical state of affairs, and Tocqueville offers what is certainly the classical explanation of it. Guizot's is the paradigmatic case of the liberal turned conservative, or more simply of the conservative liberal. The July Monarchy is also often called the "bourgeois monarchy," but in fact it corresponded to the desires of only a segment even of the bourgeoisie. There is still much argument over the precise sociological nature of this segment—whether its typical or prevailing members were landowners, state officials, professional men, or bankers; perhaps, however, there can be general agreement that they represented a new aristocracy of wealth even if that wealth may have taken forms not unlike those characteristic of the Restoration or even of the *ancien regime*. What is above all important is that, whatever their precise composition, the dominant bourgeoisie of the July Monarchy felt the weakness of their own situation in a period of accelerating social and economic change, had little faith in themselves, and could still less inspire faith in others. Insofar as Guizot had fostered the conceptions that the July Monarchy was a "bourgeois monarchy" and that the middle class was the proper political representative of the whole nation, he reaped the fruits of his own propaganda in 1848.

When taxed with the fact that even under the July Monarchy the *pays legal,* the electorate, was still restricted by high property qualifications for voting, Guizot gave the famous advice *Enrichissez-vous,* that is, become wealthy and you will get the vote. This outlook was characteristic of liberal economic doctrine as a whole, represented classically by J.-B. Say. Although, as he explains, Say by no means followed the eighteenth-century Physiocrats or Adam Smith in all their teachings, like them he stood for economic individualism, a more sophisticated individualism, in fact, than theirs and therefore a more persuasive one. But in economic theory as well as in political rationale, although liberalism was on the offensive when in opposition under the Restoration, it was driven increasingly onto the defensive when in power during the July Monarchy and when confronted, in particular, with various brands of collectivism or socialism springing up in response to the slow but steady process of industrialization that was taking place less, at first, in Paris than in such provincial cities as Bordeaux and Lyon. It is symptomatic that Sismondi, represented in the present book by an early liberal work, later abandoned liberalism and was among those who laid the foundations for the collectivist theories of such men as Louis Blanc and Auguste Blanqui who were active in the radical phase of the Revolution of 1848, a phase as brief but as important, and as damaging to liberalism, as that of the great Revolution that had begun in 1789.

PART I

Sources

1   *Jean-Joseph Mounier*

Jean-Joseph Mounier (1758-1806) was a leader of the moderates in the early years of the French Revolution. He was a discriminating admirer of Montesquieu and of the English constitution. Although suspicious of the motives and doctrines of many of those responsible for the outbreak of the revolution Mounier was by no means a counter-revolutionary. He supported reform to convert the monarchy from an absolute to a limited one. In limited or constitutional monarchy he saw the middle ground which had to be maintained between reaction to the ancien regime *on the one hand and radicalism on the other, and he sought, for example, to win over the nobility to its support. It was in this spirit also that he proposed the famous Tennis Court Oath of 1789. Later in that year he presided courageously over the Constituent Assembly when it was invaded by a hostile crowd, but he thereafter resigned his seat, withdrew to the provinces, and eventually went to Switzerland. Although he regarded his principles as having been defeated when radicalism gained ascendancy in the Constituent Assembly and in the country at large by 1791-1792, he clung to those principles and applied them in his reflections on the course of the revolution.*

SOURCES. [J.-J.] Mounier, *Considerations sur les gouvernemens, et principalement sur celui qui convient a la France,* Versailles: 1789, pp. 38-41, 44-46, 48; *Recherches sur les causes qui ont empeche les Francois de devenir libres, et sur les Moyens qui leur restent, pour acquerir la liberte,* 2 vols. in 1, Geneva: 1792, I, 1-8, II, 111-3, 147, 149-151, 168-170.

[1789]. . .It is very important for public liberty that the constitution should prevent the concentration of all power in the hands of the representatives and maintain the independence of the king. . . . To attain this important goal it is not sufficient to declare the royal assent to be necessary. The royal assent may, on some important occasions, be extremely useful; but it is impossible to deny that this device would be weak and nearly powerless if it were not supported by other means. The representatives could frustrate the royal veto by refusing to vote taxes, a measure which a king could rarely withstand. . . .

The king's veto therefore provides only a very inadequate protection for the constitution; it would certainly not be able to shelter public liberty. . .from the errors or ventures of a single assembly.

Nobody was more convinced than I of the need to vote by head and in a single body in the Estates-General of 1789. In order to give a people a constitution it is necessary to employ means which overcome all obstacles and facilitate the destruction of abuses; but I thought and still think that the same means when employed once the constitution is in force would cast doubt on it, would not allow a sound legislative process to develop, and would possess an irresistible force that might bring the greatest misfortunes on France.

I am aware that a people's constitution cannot be eternal, but it is undeniable that at least nothing should be left undone to make it as durable as possible and that the slightest disturbance in the organization of power may provoke agitation or lead to the concentration of all power in the same hands, that is to say to despotism. Once the constitution is established it must therefore be respected, and changed only after long reflection and in the presence of the clearest kind of need. . . .

The preceding reflections point to the desirability of a body interposed between the king and the representatives. This body ought to be so constituted that it could never damage public liberty but would be charged with maintaining the constitution, preventing the representatives from destroying or usurping royal authority and preventing the king from encroaching on the rights of the representatives.

The most perfect thing of this kind that I can imagine is the English peerage. The members of the House of Lords in no way resemble what we in this country call the Order of the nobility: their family does not form a class distinct and separated from the rest of the citizens; only their eldest sons can hope to become members of the upper House. . . . The Lords therefore have no interest in legislating against the general welfare, since their brothers and sons share the humiliations and misfortunes of other citizens; but they have the most powerful motives to preserve the authority of the Crown against any actions of the people's representatives and to defend the people's liberty against any actions of the Crown.

What would become of the power and dignity of the English peerage if the king were to become an absolute despot, or if the people's representatives seized executive power? In the first case they, like the rest of the citizens, would be cast into slavery; in the second they would be subordinated to the House of Commons.

The British peerage must therefore be regarded as hereditary magistrates established for the maintenance of the constitution.

This idea of heredity at first glance offends against fundamental notions of philosophy. It is said to be absurd for a man to be born a magistrate. But, as always, nothing is more dangerous in politics than to stop at the first glance. What appears to be a great evil is in certain circumstances a great boon, because it prevents even more serious evils. The magistracy of the peerage is hereditary in England, like that of the king, because this heredity offers invaluable advantages: it makes the peers independent of both the king and the people and engages their interest in maintaining the rights of the upper House.

I know about the defects of the British constitution, above all the inequities of representation in the House of Commons; but I am nevertheless convinced that no monarchical government can be established with anything approaching perfection without drawing on the principles of English government. We cannot hope to do better than the English, who have profited from the lessons of experience and spent centuries in reconciling public liberty with royal authority. . . .

Some people would like to establish within the French legislative body a Senate consisting of members elected for life instead of a hereditary magistracy. I do not think this idea feasible, as it would entirely lack the advantage of a hereditary peerage. A British peer is devoted to preserving his position which must pass to one of his children. He would be unlikely to sacrifice it for the sake of his personal interest and he would refuse to vote for laws extending the Crown's prerogatives too far, since these would destroy the authority of the peerage.

A life Senator, on the other hand, could not devote himself so much to his task. He might well use his position as a means of enriching his family, especially toward the end of his career when the desire for rest would make him indifferent to maintaining the rights of his station. It is also to be feared that the Senate would be too susceptible to ministerial influence. . . .

[1792] Citizens are free when they cannot be constrained or hindered in their actions or in the enjoyment of their property or of their industry except by laws in force at the time and established in the public interest, and never by the arbitrary authority of any man, whatever his rank or power.

If a people are to enjoy liberty, then laws, which are the most essential acts of sovereign power, must be dictated by general considerations, and not by motives of private interest; they must never have a retroactive effect, or relate to circumstances in the past or to particular persons. . . . But good laws would be useless if their protection were not accorded to the poor as well as to the rich, to the weakest as well as to the most powerful; if magistrates appointed to administer justice were not rigorously obliged to follow in their judgments the intentions contained in them.

Liberty is the highest good; it is, in fact, the principal aim of all political societies, the aim pursued in the creation of all governments; for it is clear that men did not come together under leaders except to be protected in the exercise of their rights. . . . Liberty raises the prosperity of a state to its highest level, favors the progress of the sciences, gives people energy, creates interest in [national] glory and in the general well-being of the community, and teaches people to devote themselves to the welfare of their compatriots.

Happiness cannot exist without a sense of security. In a free state this sense is born of the conviction which even the humblest man must have that his rights cannot be violated with impunity. The English use of the words SECURITY, PROPERTY when they wish to define civil or personal liberty. This definition is in fact entirely correct: all the advantages procured by liberty are expressed in these two words.

There is another kind of liberty, called political liberty, without which the first cannot endure. Montesquieu says that it consists in the conviction of being secure. It would perhaps be even better to say that political liberty is the collection of means sufficient to guarantee and maintain personal liberty, to shelter it as much as possible from the errors and passions of those who exercise sovereign power.

Whether sovereignty resides in the hands of a single individual or of a single body or even with the people as a whole, so long as it is unlimited there can be no political liberty, since nothing can prevent those who possess sovereign power from arbitrarily disposing of the lives of citizens and destroying personal liberty.

Montesquieu rightly maintains that democracy and aristocracy are not by their nature free states, and that political liberty is to be found only with moderate governments. He adds this excellent maxim: "If power is not to be abused things must be so arranged that power is countered by power."

Political liberty can have several degrees, because government can be moderated by different kind of limits; but if personal liberty is to be completely and solidly guaranteed sovereignty must be divided, that is to say, the laws or rules that it makes must be the product of agreement among several independent orders or bodies; these orders or bodies must be so organized that, while not having conflicting interests (which would throw the state into perpetual turmoil), their position is nevertheless sufficiently different for them not to be too likely to share the same passions and not to agree too readily with each other except in the public interest. Above all, any confusion must be avoided between the power which makes the laws and that which causes them to be carried out. . . . It would usually be pointless to demand observance of the laws from a despotic power which has the means of exercising it capriciously. Finally, judicial functions must be separated from the legislative and executive powers, though subject to their supervision. . . .

The liberty which I know and which I desire is not merely compatible with public peace but is positively interested in its preservation and is one of its main supports; and if, in its own defense, it is obliged to give it up for a little while it works for its return, for without peace liberty cannot distribute its benefits. It is possible for a people to enjoy civil liberty under the most absolute kind of monarchy. If the prince is enlightened he may recognize that his true interest requires him to protect the liberty of his subjects; he may refrain from arbitrary orders except in a small number of circumstances in which he may consider them to be clearly necessary; he may surround himself with men highly distinguished by their wisdom and their virtues; he may issue wise ordinances and assiduously supervise their execution; he may render justice promptly and equitably to all. It is true that civil liberty, respected by a good monarch, may be destroyed by a less prudent or less just king. . . .

If civil liberty can sometimes exist under the absolute power of a single person, it is impossible for it to be maintained when absolute power rests with the people, or with a large part of the people. Such a sovereign is incapable of subjecting itself to the rules of prudence and justice which a monarch is often obliged to observe by the very nature of his position. The government least favorable to liberty would therefore be a pure democracy, that is to say, supreme and unlimited power in the hands of the people. . . . All unlimited and indivisible sovereignty is a true despotism; the multitude is the most capricious and cruel of all despots. Even supposing that the acts of government were always the result of the wishes of the majority of citizens, all those excluded from the suffrage and all those who were in the minority would be exposed to the most crushing tyranny. Since each individual may at one time or another be in the minority, in a state where all sovereign power rested without restriction with the people there would be neither political liberty nor personal liberty. . . .

What an appalling idea of liberty one must have to believe that it exists in France!. . . I know of no rights, natural or civil, that. . .a Frenchman could now claim to be able to exercise freely, or at any rate of which he could not be deprived at any moment with impunity.

It is sufficient to recall the definition of personal liberty to realize that the revolution has destroyed it. Nobody could maintain in good faith that anyone in France is secure either in his person or in his property.

Security of property and persons cannot exist without a precise and rigorous administration of justice: but the judiciary order established since the revolution is more defective than any that has ever existed among any known people, not excepting even the Athenians whose tribunals were manned by citizens chosen by lot; for chance may produce just and enlightened men, and a man who owed his temporary functions to chance retained his independence of mind. An ignorant or not entirely honest man who receives a judgeship for life may acquire knowledge and may often find his own interest coinciding with the principles of equity; but how can impartial justice be dispensed by courts composed of officials nominated by the people for a period of six years from among a large number of eligible persons? Nominations determined by birth or by patronage are infinitely less dangerous. A judge who is the slave of a princely court is a hundred times preferable to a judge who is the slave of the multitude. . . . The sword of a single tyrant is much less to be feared than the clubs and daggers of a populace in a frenzy. . . .

Most Frenchmen have desired a free government for a long time; but since there appeared to be no possibility of obtaining it nobody took the trouble to study political affairs or to take note of the effects of various institutions in the course of history. . . .

In politics the only systems that are simple and easy to understand are unfortunately those that tend either to despotism or to anarchy. . . .A wide knowledge of history and of human nature is necessary to appreciate the advantages of a balance of powers and the need to introduce into a limited monarchy an aristocratic element in order to protect the throne from public agitation. Most writers and scholars had neither the time nor the inclination to embark on a new kind of studies. Even those who up to this time had devoted themselves to subjects entirely unconnected with government insisted on getting in on the act when they saw so many ignorant men set themselves up as publicists. They thought that the most convenient doctrine. . .was that of equality and popular sovereignty. They were saved from the embarrassment of

having to provide proof of their doctrines by having on their side
the vanity of their audience. . . .

Finally, the majority of those who wanted to learn some politics
preferred the shortest and simplest course, the one that its author's
great reputation had elevated to a collection of oracles: I refer to
the *Social Contract,* the worst book ever written on government. . . .

J.-J. Rousseau drew the principles of his *Social Contract* from the
writers of the English republic. He fell so absurdly in love with
democracy that, while purporting to trace the principles of all
forms of government, he did not succeed in writing a single word
that was not democratic; for he never refers to any sovereign other
than the people, or to any law other than the general will which,
according to him, cannot be represented. . . .

Corrupted peoples can scarcely be expected to have sound ideas
on liberty. When men tainted by the luxury and vices of servitude
wish to become free they usually pitch themselves into the most
unrestrained license. . . . It seems therefore to be the sad fate of
peoples hardly ever to be able to attain political liberty except
after a long series of misfortunes, and to disdain it when they have
the opportunity of seizing it. . . .

We have seen the French, formerly celebrated for their gentle
manners, engaged since July 1789 in acts of cruelty which one
would not have thought possible in Europe at the end of the
eighteenth century. People have not been slow to infer that,
beneath its apparent lightheartedness, this was really a savage
nation; and they have not allowed for the fact that a complete
dissolution of government would lead to the same crimes everywhere. No country could escape from the ravages that are
inevitably produced when the maxims of the absolute equality of
all men and popular sovereignty are preached in the midst of a
general upheaval.

2   *Jacques Mallet du Pan*

Jacques Mallet du Pan (1749-1800), a native of Switzerland living in France at the time of the Revolution, was politically close to Mounier and the group of moderates but, unlike Mounier, he remained politically active after leaving France when the cause of constitutional monarchy was lost. He became first a confidential emissary of Louis XVI to the powers at war with France in 1792 and subsequently, in England, an adviser to the prince who later became Louis XVIII and to other royalist emigres. This counterrevolutionary activity is reflected in his later writings, which in their vindictiveness contrast both with Mounier's reflections and with his own earlier more detached tone. In the first of the extracts that follow, Mallet du Pan philosophizes on the rights of man; in the second he outlines the ideas held in 1789 by the group to which he and Mounier belonged; the third is a commentary on the dissolution of the Constituent Assembly in 1791; the last two are self-explanatory.

[From the *Mercure de France,* 1789.] The rights of man insure to him the free exercise of his faculties, physical and moral; whence results in reality an inequality of rights proportional to those of his faculties. The superiority of power, of intelligence, and dexterity, give rise to the dominion of one man over another, and so long as the human species remains in that primitive state, it remains subject to differences which Nature herself has made between individuals. Thus the bushes bow beneath the oak, and the herrings are devoured by the whales. Take this example of the rights of nature.

Society substitutes a conventional right; it levels inequalities by the establishment of political equality: this could never be anything but ideal without laws which determine its application and insure its maintenance. These laws alone are the rights of the

SOURCE. Mallet du Pan, *Memoirs and Correspondence Illustrative of the History of the French Revolution* (ed. A. Sayous), 2 vols., London: 1852, I, 179-181, 189-193, 246-248, II, 157-161, 247-251.

social man and those of the community of which he is a member. If he arrogated others, such a pretension would become general—society would be dissolved.

The rights of the individual are therefore inseparable from those of the citizen, since it is only by this latter right that he is removed from the natural superiority of physical and moral powers. Positive laws determine his condition, his prerogatives, and their limits: there cannot now remain to him, under penalty of entering into opposition with his fellow-men, any other rights than those which have been sanctioned by general society. Consequently to declare the rights of man is to declare the laws a futility; for truth itself does not bind the citizen, except in so far as it is related to an actual institution: the noblest maxims will never have in the social system the force of a police regulation. . . .

When, in 1688, the English drew up their famous bill of rights, they were perfectly well acquainted with the rights of man in general; for ten years in succession they had developed them under the reign of Charles I. . . . However, the Parliament contented itself with declaring the laws whose violations it repaired, and the new laws which it enacted.

The Americans have followed another course; but it is in their charters, and not in their parliamentary declarations, that the present generation or the following will find the principles of their liberty and the means of defending it.

[From the *Mercure de France,* 1791.] In advocating the union of the three estates in a primary assembly, this party aimed at defending them against the attacks of the communes, by a conditional union, a positive and obligatory treaty. Such was the literal meaning of the Dauphine manifestoes, drawn up by the three orders in common; sacred, consequently, in the eyes of all the deputies of the province, and placing the limitation of sacrifices under the safeguard of the most solemn convention.

In restoring to the communes the measure of authority, strength and independence, which would have balanced them against the royal power and the first two estates of the monarchy, this third party had no idea of their swamping the public sovereignty and smoothing a path to democracy by destroying pre-existent institutions root and branch. It aimed at reforming the clergy without degrading it, at diminishing its opulence without despoiling it, at extending the blessings of tolerance without stripping the religion of twenty-two millions of Frenchmen of the rights of a national creed.

It would have considered itself guilty of usurpation and tyranny, had it laid a finger on individual property under the pretext of public need; it never so much as conceived that philosophic policy which supplies want of skill by a daring injustice, and which ruins whole classes of citizens to save the public weal.

Considering the National Assembly as a constituent deputation, subordinate to its commission and to the free consent of the sovereign, it recognized its right to organize, in concert with the King, the institution of the fundamental powers of the State, and consequently disavowed its competence to administer any of such powers.

Desiring a revolution according to reason and justice, not by intervention of a furious multitude and the crimes of anarchy, it did not suspect that this would be conjured up without occasion, to obtain a pretext for investing the constituent body with the totality of public powers, legislation, governmental administration, command, organization of the army, police, superintendence of the finances in detail, and judicial power.

They opposed two barriers to the acts of this unexampled sovereignty—the right of ratification by the people, and the right of ratification by the King.

According to the system of this party, and in conformity with the immutable basis of every monarchy that would combine the liberty with the wisdom of laws, and the stability of institutions with public tranquillity, the legislative functions were divided, and the executive power strictly concentrated in the person of the monarch.

The hereditary succession to the crown and its inviolability in the reigning family were declared, without any assumption of the right of founding them. Not only the power of the supreme chief, independent and sole executive, was recognized in the sovereign, but also the attributes and the functions of royalty. Consequently, he formally continued an integral portion of the legislative power, in virtue of the necessity of his sanction, and the independence of his absolute negative. . . . Supreme administrator of justice, he was not excluded from all participation in the choice of magistrates and the prosecution of national crimes. Supreme chief of the executive, his subordinate functionaries were not independent of his legal orders, remaining subject exclusively to nomination by the people and the sole judgment of the legislative body. His authority over the forces of the State was not neutralized by an army absolutely independent, under the title of National Guard, he himself being deprived of the power of even disbanding a regiment in the army of the line. The responsibility of his ministers was to be determined so as to protect law and freedom without enervating the action of government, without so subordinating these agents to the legislature that they should become the slaves of a few demagogues, to bruise with their chains both the King and the nation.

In suppressing the representation according to orders the higher classes of society were indemnified in those distinctions which offend neither liberty, property, nor political equality. It was thought preferable thus to regulate and limit the already existing influence of rank, in order to guard against the disturbances which accompany their inevitable re-establishment, to preserve the State from the unavoidable and immediate clashing of monarch and people, to interest these intermediate classes in public liberty and the maintenance of the constitution—to temper, in fine, the insolent and base aristocracy of riches without birth, without merit, without honourable emulation, without national feeling. . . .

For the all-powerful consideration that France is an agricultural country, and that the owners of land alone possess a sovereign interest in the maintenance of law and order, bear the chief burden of public expenditure, and are exclusively endowed with the character of independence essential to the delegates of the nation, to them alone was confided the function of representing it, and the power of constituting its assembled delegates a House of Commons.

The fuel of demagogism, the plague of the abuse of eloquence in an assembly, the insensate excitement of debate, the tyranny of a majority, and the inevitable usurpation of a single assembly, the exclusive representative of the pretended general will, were counteracted by establishing a regulating body, a higher house reserved for the elective deputies of the clergy and the nobility, and for citizens of whatever rank, eminent for great services, or large property, called by the King to this senatorial magistracy. . . .

[From the *Mercure de France,* 1791.] Only by denying positive and authenticated facts, the Constituent Assembly hides from itself that its dogmas and operations annihilate all religious principle; leave our morals in the lowest state of abasement; every vice at full liberty; the right of possession attacked and sapped at its very foundation; our military and naval forces in a worse condition than when the rule of the Assembly commenced; that it has shaken, if not annihilated, all military organization; that it has left our finance ruined—our national debt considerably augmented, the annual deficit increased by one-half, according to the most favourable calculations—the imposts in arrear suspended, their principle attacked by the daring of an absolutely new system, of which the immediate consequence has been to accustom the people to believe themselves freed from taxes. It cannot hide from itself that our influence and standing in Europe are lowered, that our trade is less flourishing, our manufactures are less productive, our population is less numerous; that the amount of labour has decreased in proportion with the national wealth; that it has caused the circulating medium to disappear, and dissipated an enormous fund of public capital; finally, that our internal police, notwithstanding its numerous overseers, is more oppressive and less effective than it was before the Revolution. . . .

To appreciate the conduct of our chief legislators, we must dismiss the sophistries with which they constantly fascinate the vulgar, by contrasting the present condition of France with the disastrous results of the most horrible despotism. That is a false assumption, to which deceivers and dupes always take care to recur. An immense number of citizens has no more taste for the new system than for the old; and it is not on the reformation of the first that those reproaches fall, with which they overwhelm the second. To conquer their disapproval, it must be proved, that without the doings of the Assembly, without the public and private calumnies they have caused, France would never have obtained liberty, protection of property, and of personal security, which is the first condition of good government; peace, which is its sign; political equality, abundance, strength, order, universal respect. It must be proved, besides, that the Assembly had not the option of other institutions—that no middle course was possible, and that it proclaimed the only suitable government, because no other offend such certain advantages or a future more evidently satisfactory.

[From a memorandum for Louis XVIII, 1795.] It is the general conviction, that it will be requisite first of all, to repass through the forge of 1781 in order to arrive at a good monarchy. Any other transition offers too many difficulties and dangers to men intimidated by two years of ferocious tyranny, which has made the people lose the very feeling of its power, absorbing it in that of the power of its oppressors.

Generally speaking, it is but too true that the great majority of the French nation, having taken part in the Revolution through errors of conduct or of opinion, it will never surrender at discretion to the old authority and its representatives: we need only enter into the human heart to be convinced of this fact. The national vanity, maddened for three consecutive years, wounded but not stifled by the system of terror, revolts equally at the idea of a pardon, especially when offered by the legitimate heads of the monarchy, who have not the power to re-establish it, and to a mass of men who consider themselves alone in a position to become its restorers. I may add, it is impossible to conceal that a portion of the principles of the day has survived the horrors of the Revolution, and that the present generation, infected with this leaven, can only deliver itself from it in course of time, and with a firm and enlightened government. . . .

It will be asked what course of conduct. . . ought the King and the august Princes of the house of Bourbon to follow?

The reply to this question would be as complicated as the difficulties which surrounded its solution. Not one method—nor two—nor three, but a concurrence of resources would, perhaps, be demanded by such unprecedented circumstances.

Two broad plans present themselves—either to incite civil war in the interior, for the re-establishment of monarchy; or to profit by the existing elements for its restoration, do no more than second their action, and combine with them to endow their development with the strength of union. . . .

The character of the age, the ravages of the revolution, the weakening of all energy, have suppressed in France (as in all Europe) those heroic and deep sentiments of fidelity, attachment, exalted loyalty, which determine men to great sacrifices, electrify them rapidly, and rally them without reflection. There is not at the present day a Frenchman in the interior who does not calculate his duties by his danger.

I venture to affirm, therefore, that the most eminent, the most honourable chief entering France without means, or without having created beforehand such as might be seized and employed at the moment of his appearance, will find himself either deserted, or incapable of making head and contending against the resources of the Convention.

It would then be necessary, I repeat, before taking the field openly, to create these means, and render them of sufficient importance to become means of war and sustained resistance. Nothing is easier than to foment and produce some local insurrections. Such sudden strokes, which have been far too much relied upon these five years, are pernicious, unless their morrow has been provided for. Experience has proved, and will prove everlastingly, the ease with which such movements can be crushed. . . .

So long as the Convention abstains from peopling either the prisons or the tomb, so long as it does not make its yoke felt intolerably, a revolt of any importance is not to be expected. A nation reduced for the past five months to living on from two to four ounces of bread a day, to paying sixty francs for a pair of shoes, and to a conflict with hourly destitution, will remain quiet under usurpers, whenever it has not before its eyes prisons, or revolutionary committees, or guillotines, and so long as it does not despair of a turn of fortune.

No royalist party exists; now, without a royalist party, there is no war. To form such a party, no elements except interest and sentiments of the most general kind, common to the partisans of monarchical government. The first study should therefore be devoted to this interest and these sentiments, and the plan of conduct, whatever it be, based on these data.

I take the liberty of respectfully soliciting a distrust of visionaries and men carried away by party-spirit. The former represent France as opening its arms to receive the old *regime;* the others take fright at any constitutional or limited system as at an irreparable evil. These two methods of viewing matters are equally false in fact and in hypothesis. The vast majority of the French repudiate the old *regime;* but, whatever may be its desire for another system; that is—will be—and can be, nothing but a transition from the Republic to a monarchy.

[From Mallet du Pan's Introduction to his *Correspondance pour servir a l'histoire du republicanisme francais,* 1796.] It would be erroneous to suppose that the spirit of republicanism has sprung up in France only since the revolution. The independence of manners, the relaxation of duties, the inconsistency of authority; the impetuous heat of opinions in a country, where the want of reflection transforms them immediately into prejudices; finally, the American inoculation had infused this spirit into all the reasoning classes. Most of the malcontents in France proclaimed themselves democrats, as most of them do at present in the rest of Europe. The people alone remained strangers to this effervescence. A Frenchman hates all superiority so much, that by effacing that of the King, he became incapable of supporting any. The system of equality drove away that of liberty; the balance of powers seemed an aristocracy: each busy-body said to himself: "I shall participate in the command, and will not recognize that of any one." There was, therefore, no medium in ideas, nor discretion in enterprises: they steered towards the republic, under the monarchical flag, and when in 1791, the breakers frightened the pilots, they wished to resuscitate royalty:—that was only a carcase pierced with a thousand poniards. . . .

Meantime, while theorists are searching for the philosopher's stone of speculative politics, society gradually crumbles away, and its ashes settle at the bottom of the crucible. As nothing presents fewer difficulties than the perfecting of what is imaginary, all restless spirits expand, and move freely in this ideal world. This is one of the principal causes of the success which has attended the Gallican innovations. They leave far behind them all known systems of free government, and intoxicate the brains of fools, while they inflame the passions of the mob. People begin with curiosity, and end with enthusiasm.

No man who feels the dignity of his nature will ever fail to recognize the claims of the human race, or the respect which social liberty has a right to demand from governments. Nature certainly never intended that nations should, like flocks, be the property of those whom necessity has charged with the duty of protecting them. The government of Morocco is, no doubt, a blessing when compared with the rule of five-hundred revolutionary atheists; but reason will ever invoke the absolutism of justice; and there can be no justice without inviolable laws; no inviolable laws without a positive constitution to act as their safeguard.

This need, however, varies infinitely, according to centuries, nations, physical and moral conditions. To attempt to satisfy it on an unvarying system, is to remould the bed of iron in which a tyrant stretched the limbs of his victims. To begin the legislation of a state by isolated political laws, is to lay the keystone of the arch before building the edifice.

Above and beyond all else, the people are deeply interested in the civil and judicial laws. . . . The civil and judicial laws alone form the citizen; for they embrace him in all respects, and defend him in all his legal actions. Political laws enclose him merely in an eccentric circumference; they regulate public power far more than liberty itself, of which they form the complement, by the security they ensure to the people for the maintenance of civil institutions. . . .

I will add that, on the day when men of property and character shall have weight in the government, their first need will be to overturn it, in order to revert to the only protection possible in a state like France, that of a monarch who defends the laws against a million usurpers, without having the power of becoming one himself.

3   Antoine-Nicolas de Condorcet

Antoine-Nicolas de Condorcet (1743-1794) was one 'Philosophes' of the eighteenth century still living in 1789. Best known for this Sketch for a Historical Picture of the Progress of the Human Mind, *in which he brought the eighteenth-century Idea of Progress to its highest and clearest expression, Condorcet was a first-rate mathematician in his own right and served as permanent secretary to the Academy of Sciences. Like all the Philosophes a critic of the ancien regime, Condorcet was prepared to go farther politically than Mounier and Mallet du Pan and to abandon the idea of constitutional monarchy, as witness his membership not only of the Legislative Assembly of 1791 to 1792 but also of the Constitutional Convention which was charged with the task of producing a republican constitution. Condorcet was nevertheless a man of political moderation who eventually committed suicide to escape the executioners of the radical faction who gained control of the Convention. The extract that follows is from a report presented to the Legislative Assembly in April, 1792 on behalf of its committee on education. It is of particular interest because education was, on the one hand, a subject of central concern to the Philosophes and, on the other hand, a field of activity in which the Revolution was very thorough in replacing the institutions of the ancien regime* Condorcet's report provides the link. Most of the measures recommended on the basis of the principles outlined in this report were subsequently adopted.

SOURCE. "Condorcet's Report on Education," No. 73, in John Hall Stewart, ed., *A Documentary Survey of the French Revolution*, New York: Macmillan, 1951, pp. 347-355, 357, 361, 368-9. Copyright by the Macmillan Company, 1951; reprinted by permission of the publisher.

Gentlemen,

To offer all individuals of the human race the means of providing for their needs, of assuring their well-being, of knowing and exercising their rights, of understanding and performing their duties;

To assure each of them the facility of perfecting his skill, of rendering himself capable of the social functions to which he has a right to be summoned, of developing to the fullest extent the talents with which Nature has endowed him; and thereby to establish among citizens an actual equality, and to effect the realization of the political equality recognized by law:

Such must be the primary aim of national education; and from this point of view it is a task of probity for the government.

To direct teaching in such a manner that perfecting of the arts increases the pleasures of the generality of the citizens, and the comfort of those who devote themselves to it; that a greater number of men may become capable of performing the duties necessary to society, and that the ever-increasing progress of enlightenment may open an inexhaustible source of aid according to our needs, of remedies according to our ills, of means of individual happiness and of common prosperity;

Finally, to cultivate in each generation the physical, intellectual, and moral faculties, and thereby to contribute to this general and gradual improvement of the human race, should be the ultimate aim towards which every social institution must be directed.

Such, moreover, must be the object of education; and it is a duty imposed on the government by the common interest of society, by that of all humanity.

But, in considering from these two points of view the immense task imposed upon us, we have felt from the very first that there was one part of the general system of education which it was possible to separate without harm to the whole, and that it was even necessary to do so in order to hasten the realization of the new system: that is, the distribution and general organization of establishments for public education. . . .

We have felt that in this plan of general organization our prime care should be to render education on the one hand as equal, as universal, on the other as complete as circumstances permit; that the education that it is possible to extend to all should be given to all equally; but not to refuse higher education to any part of the citizens because it is impossible to share it with the total population; to establish the one because it is useful to those who receive it, and the other because it is useful even to those who do not receive it.

Since the prime requisite of all education is that only the truth be taught, the establishments consecrated by the government must be as independent as possible of all political authority; since, however, such independence cannot be absolute, it results from the same principle that they must be rendered dependent only upon the assembly of the representatives of the people, because of all powers it is the least corruptible, the least likely to be influenced by particular interests, the most subject to the influence of the general opinion of enlightened men, and, above all, since it is the one from which all changes necessarily emanate, it is hence the least inimical to the progress of enlightenment, the least opposed to the improvements which such progress is to effect.

Finally, we have observed that education must not forsake individuals when they leave school, that it must encompass all ages, that there is no age at which it is not useful and possible to learn, and that this later education is even more necessary because that of childhood is restricted within the narrowest limits. Therein lies one of the principal causes of the ignorance in which the poorer class of society are plunged today; the possibility of obtaining a primary education is greater than that of preserving its advantages.

We wish that henceforth not a single man in the realm may be able to say, "The law assures me an entire equality of rights, but I am denied the means of knowing them. I must depend only upon the law; but my ignorance renders me dependent upon everything around me. In my childhood I was well informed concerning what I needed to know; but, forced to work for my living, I soon lost those first rudiments; and there remains to me only the grief of feeling in my ignorance not the will of Nature but the injustice of society."

We believe that the government should say to the poor citizen:

"The lot of your parents enabled you to obtain only the most indispensable knowledge, but you are assured of easy means of preserving and extending it. If Nature has given you talents, you may develop them, and they will not be lost either to you or to the *Patrie.*"

Thus, education must be universal, that is to say, it must extend to all citizens. It must be shared as equally as the necessary limitations of expense, the distribution of population, and the greater or lesser amount of time that children may devote to it permit. It must, in its several degrees, comprise the entire system of human knowledge, and assure to men of all ages the facility of preserving their knowledge or of acquiring new knowledge.

Finally, no public power is to have either the authority or even the influence, to hinder the development of new truths, the teaching of theories contrary to its special policies or its temporary interests. . . .

In the primary schools each individual will learn whatever is necessary for his personal guidance and for the enjoyment of his full rights. Such education will suffice also for those who profit from the lessons intended to render men capable of the simplest public duties to which it is desirable that every citizen be summoned, such as juryman or municipal official. . . .

The secondary schools are intended for children whose families can do without their work for a longer time, and can devote to their education a greater number of years, or even some money.

Each district, and also each town of 4,000 inhabitants, will have one of such secondary schools. An arrangement similar to that mentioned in connection with the primary schools will prevent inequality in the distribution of these establishments. The course of study will be the same in all; but each school will have one, two, or three teachers, according to the number of pupils expected to attend.

Some elements of mathematics, natural history, applied chemistry, a more extensive development of the principles of ethics and social science, and elementary instruction in commerce will constitute the basis of their curriculum. . . .

The third grade of instruction comprises the elements of all human knowledge. Such instruction, considered as a part of general education, is absolutely complete.

It includes what is necessary to enable a man to prepare himself to perform public duties which require the highest degree of enlightenment, or to devote himself successfully to the most profound studies. There teachers for secondary schools will be trained; likewise masters for primary schools, already prepared in the secondary schools, will receive further training.

The number of institutes has been fixed at 110, and they will be established in all the departments.

In them will be taught not only what is useful to know as a man, as a citizen, no matter what profession one may intend to follow, but also all that may be needed for each of the major divisions of the professions, such as agriculture, the mechanical arts, military science; and even such medical knowledge as is necessary for simple practitioners, midwives, and veterinarians will be added.

* * *

Several motives have determined the type of preference accorded the mathematics and physical sciences. In the first place,. . . .even the elementary study of these sciences is the surest means of developing intellectual faculties, of learning to reason correctly and to analyze ideas effectively. Doubtless it is possible, by application to literature, grammar, history, political science, to philosophy in general, to acquire precision, method, a sound and profound logic, and still be ignorant of the natural sciences. Great examples have proved this; but elementary knowledge of these same subjects has not this advantage; it makes use of reason, but it does not develop it. That is because in the natural sciences the ideas are simpler, more rigorously circumscribed, the language is more perfect, the same words express the same ideas more exactly. The elements constitute a real part of the science, restricted within narrow limits, but complete in itself. Again, they afford reason a means of practicing which is within the grasp of the greater number of intelligences, especially in youth. . . . These sciences are a remedy for prejudices and narrow-mindedness which is, if not surer, at least more universal than philosophy itself. They are useful in all professions, and it is easy to see how much more so they would be if they were more uniformly diffused. Those who follow the progress of the sciences see the time approaching when the practical utility of their application will reach an extent which no one would have dared hope for, when the progress of the physical sciences is to bring about a happy revolution in the arts; and the surest means of hastening this revolution is to spread such knowledge among among all classes of society and to facilitate the means of acquiring it.

Finally, we have yielded to the general attitude of mind which, in Europe, seems to incline more and more to these sciences with ever-increasing intensity. We feel that, as a consequence of the progress of the human race, these studies which offer its activity an eternal and inexhaustible sustenance are becoming the more necessary as the improvement in the social order must leave less scope for ambition or greed; that in a country where at last it is desired to unite peace and liberty by eternal bonds, it ought to be possible, without tedium, without sinking into idleness, to consent to be only a man and a citizen; and that it is important to turn towards useful objectives that need for action, that thirst for glory for which the state of a well-governed society does not afford a vast enough field of action, and thus to substitute the desire to enlighten men for the desire to dominate them. . . .

You owe the French nation an education on a level with the spirit of the eighteenth century, with that philosophy which, while enlightening the present generation, presages, prepares, and already anticipates the superior intelligence to which the necessary progress of the human race is leading future generations.

Such are our principles; and it is according to that philosophy, untrammeled, independent of all authority, free from all old habits, that we have chosen and classified the subjects of public education. According to that same philosophy we have considered the moral and political sciences an essential part of common education.

In fact, how is it possible to hope ever to raise the ethical standards of a people unless the standards of the men who are able to enlighten it, who are destined to guide it, are based on a rigorous and exact analysis of the moral sentiments, of the ideas which derive from them, and of the principles of justice which they produce?

. . .In order that citizens may love the laws without ceasing to be really free, in order that they may preserve that independence of mind without which devotion to liberty is only a passion and not a virtue, they must know those principles of natural justice, those essential rights of man, of which the laws are only the development or the application. . . . In loving laws they must know how to judge them.

Never will a people enjoy a stable, assured liberty if instruction in political science is not universal, if it is not independent of all social institutions, if the enthusiasm aroused in the souls of citizens is not guided by reason, if they are capable of being inspired by anything but truth, if, while attaching men by habit, by imagination, by sentiment to its constitution, its laws, and its liberty, you do not prepare for them, by a general education, the means of achieving a more perfect constitution, of giving them better laws, and of attaining a more complete liberty. For it is the same with liberty, with equality, with these great political reflections as with the other sciences; there exists in the order of things possible a final limit for which Nature wishes us to be able constantly to strive, but which it is impossible for us ever to attain. . . .

The principles of morality taught in the schools and the institutes will be those which, founded on natural sentiments and on reason, are common to all men. The Constitution, by recognizing the right of each individual to choose his religion, by establishing complete equality among all the inhabitants of France, does not permit the introduction into public education of any teaching which, by excluding the children of part of the citizens, would destroy the equality of social advantages, and give to particular dogmas an advantage contrary to freedom of opinion. It is, then, absolutely necessary to separate ethics from the principles of any special religion, and not to permit in public education the teaching of any religious creed.

Each religion must be taught in its own temples by its own ministers. Parents, whatever their opinion concerning the necessity of one religion or another, may, accordingly, without reluctance, send their children to the national schools; and the government will not have usurped rights over consciences under pretext of enlightening and guiding them.

Besides, how important it is to base morality on the principles of reason alone!. . .

We have given the name *lycee* to the fourth grade of instruction. In this grade all the subjects will be taught in their entirety. In the *lycees* scholars will prepare themselves—those who make of the cultivation of their minds, of the perfecting of their own faculties one of the occupations of their lives, those who intend to follow one of the professions in which great success can be attained only by assiduous study of one or more of the sciences. The professors also will be prepared here. It is by means of these establishments that each generation may transmit to the following generation what it has received from the preceding one, and what it has been able to add thereto. . . .

After having freed education from all kinds of authority, let us be careful not to subject it to public opinion, which it should anticipate, correct, and form, but neither follow nor obey. . . . This independence of all external authority, in which we have placed public education, need alarm no one, since any abuse would be corrected instantly by the legislative power, which has direct authority over the entire system of education. Does not the existence of free instruction and of independently established learned societies also oppose to this abuse a power of opinion so much the more important because, under a popular constitution, no institution can exist unless public opinion adds its force to that of the law? Besides, there is a final authority which, in all things pertaining to the sciences, nothing can resist: the general opinion of enlightened men in all Europe, an opinion which it is impossible to mislead or to corrupt. . . . It is, in a word, for savants, for men of letters, for philosophers, a sort of anticipated posterity, whose judgments are as impartial and almost as sure, and a supreme power, from whose control they cannot attempt to escape.

Finally, independence of instruction is, in a sense, a part of the rights of the human race. Since man has received from Nature a perfectibility whose unknown limits extend—if they even exist—far beyond what we can yet conceive, since knowledge of new truths is for him the sole means of developing this happy faculty, which is the source of his happiness and of his glory, what power could have the right to say to him: "This is what you need to know: this is as far as you may go"? Since truth alone is useful, since every error is evil, by what right would any power, whatever it be, dare to determine wherein lies truth, wherein lies error?

Besides, any power which would forbid the teaching of any opinion contrary to that which has served as a basis for the established laws, would be directly attacking freedom of thought, would frustrate the aim of every social institution, the perfecting of the laws, which is the necessary consequences of the difference of opinions and the progress of enlightenment.

On the other hand, what authority could prescribe the teaching of a doctrine that is contrary to the principles which have guided the legislators? There is only one means of avoiding, on the one hand, a superstitious respect for existing laws and, on the other, an indirect attack which, made against such laws in the name of one of the authorities instituted by them, could weaken the respect of the citizens for all law. This means is the absolute independence of opinions in all teaching beyond the elementary schools. There would then exist voluntary submission to the laws and the teaching of the means of correcting their defects, of rectifying their errors, without this liberty of opinion's being in any way harmful to public order, without this respect for the law's shackling the intelligence or arresting the progress of enlightenment and sanctioning errors. . . .

Moreover, the French Constitution itself makes such independence a strict duty. It recognizes that the Nation has the inalienable and imprescriptible right to reform all its laws. It wishes then that, in national education, everything should be submitted to a rigorous examination. It has given no law an irrevocability for more than ten years. It wishes then that the principles of all laws should be discussed, that all political theories be taught and contested, that no system of social organization be presented to enthusiasm or to prejudices as the object of a superstitious veneration, but that all should be presented to the reason as divers combinations among which it has the right to choose.

4   *Destutt de Tracy*

Destutt de Tracy (1754-1836) was a leader of the school of Ideologues *who, for a variety of reasons good and bad, attracted Napoleon Bonaparte's disfavor. For this reason the manuscript of the book from which the following extract is taken was banned from publication in France during Napoleon's reign, and the first printing was therefore the American one, anonymously translated, used here. Under the Restoration a number of pirated and inaccurate French editions appeared until Destutt de Tracy issued an authorized French version in 1828. In this work Destutt de Tracy analyzes and comments on Montesquieu's* Esprit des lois *(1748) systematically, Book by Book, from a moral and psychological at least as much as from a political point of view. The argument in the extract printed here is interesting among other reasons, because it leads the author to prefer the United States constitution to the British one, which Montesquieu had so much admired.*

BOOK XI OF THE LAWS WHICH ESTABLISH PUBLIC LIBERTY, IN RELATION TO THE CONSTITUTION

. . . In this book . . . the degree of liberty which may be enjoyed under each constitution of government is examined: that is to say. . . the effects produced on the liberties of the citizens by the laws forming the constitution of the state. Such laws are those only which regulate the distribution of political power; for the constitution of a society is nothing more than the collection of rules determining the nature, extent, and limits, of the authorities ruling it; so that when these rules are to be united into a single body of laws, serving as the bond of the political edifice, the first precaution to be taken, is not to admit any thing irreconcilable with the objects proposed to be secured; without which precaution

SOURCE. Destutt de Tracy, Antoine Louis Claude, comte, *A Commentary and Review of Montesquieu's Spirit of Laws*. . ., Philadelphia: 1811, pp. 94-107.

it is not exactly a *constitution*, but an expedient, calculated for a greater or a less considerable portion of the general body of the nation.

To know what influence the organization of society has on the liberty of its members, we should perfectly understand what is meant by liberty. The word liberty, like all others intended to express abstract ideas of a very general nature, is often taken in a multitude of different acceptations, which are so many particular parts of its comprehensive signification; thus we say, a man has become free, when he has finished an enterprize, in which he had been wholly occupied; when he has given up a slavish office; when he has renounced a station, which imposed responsible duties on him; when he has broken the yoke of certain passions, or connexions, which kept him in subjection; when he has escaped from a prison; when he has withdrawn himself from the dominions of a tyrannical government: we likewise say, the liberty of thinking, speaking, acting, writing; that his speech, respiration, and all his movements are free, when nothing constrains him in these respects: then all these particular faculties of liberty are ranged into classes, forming different groups according to their several natures; such as physical, moral, natural, civil, and political liberty; whence it happens, that when forming a general idea of liberty, every one composes it of that kind of liberty, to which he attaches the greatest importance, of a freedom from those constraints against which he is the most prejudiced, and which appear to him the most insupportable; some make it to consist in virtue, in indifference, or in a kind of impassibility, like those stoics who pretended that their sages remained free, even when in chains; others place it in society; others in competency and ease, or in a state unconnected with and independent of any social ties; others again pretend, that to be free is to live under certain forms of government, or generally under one that is moderate and enlightened. All these opinions are just, according to the sense in which liberty is understood; but in none is it seen in all its forms, nor is its proper character embraced in any of their definitions. Let us examine what these different kinds of liberty possess in common, and in what they severally resemble each other; for it is in this way only we can approach the general ideas, abstracted from all the particular ideas which are comprehended therein.

If we consider it attentively, we shall perceive that one property common to all descriptions of liberty, is that it procures for the individual enjoying it, the exercise of his will in a greater extent that if deprived of that enjoyment; therefore, the idea of liberty, in its most abstract form, as well as in its greatest extent, is nothing more than the idea of the power to do that which the mind wills; and in general, to be free is to be enabled to do what we please.

Hence, we perceive that liberty is applicable only to beings endowed with will; and when we say of water that it runs more freely when the obstacles opposed to its passage are taken away, or that a wheel turns more freely when the friction retarding it is diminished it is by comparison we express ourselves, because we presuppose that the water inclines or possesses a quality which disposes it to run, and the wheel a like disposition to turn; or that such is the necessary effect in given circumstances.

For the same reason, this question so much debated. . . . *Is our will free?* should never be urged, for it is an abuse of terms; liberty only relates to the will when formed, and not before the will exists: what has given rise to an enquiry of this kind is, that on particular occasions the motives acting upon us are so powerful, that they determine us immediately to will one thing in preference to or rather than another, and then it is said, we will irresistably [*sic*] or are necessitated to will; while in other circumstances, the motives not being so strong, or acting with less impulsion, leave us the power of deliberation, to reflect on and weigh them in our minds; in this state, we think we possess the power either to resist or to obey those impulses, and to take one determination in preference to another, solely because we will it; but this is an illusion, for however weak a motive may be, it necessarily determines our will, unless it be balanced by a more powerful motive, and then this is as necessarily determined as the other would have been, if alone; we will or we do not will, but we cannot will to will; and if we could, there would yet be an antecedent cause of this will, and this cause would be beyond the range of the will, as are all those which cause it; and therefore we must conclude that liberty exists only after the will; and in consequence of its unrestrained exercise; or that liberty is no more than the power of executing the will. I ask the reader's pardon, for this metaphysical discussion on the nature of liberty, but it will soon be perceived, that it is neither inappropriate nor useless. It is impossible to speak intelligibly on the interests of men without a previous and due understanding of their faculties; if there be any thing more materially deficient than another, in the writings of the great man on which I comment, it is particularly in this preliminary study, and we may perceive how vague the ideas are which he presents to us of liberty, although he had devoted three chapters to that particular subject. . . .

Liberty, in the most general acceptation of the word, is nothing else than the power of executing the will, and accomplishing our desires; now the nature of every being endowed with will, is such that this faculty of willing causes his happiness or unhappiness, he is happy when his desires are accomplished, and unhappy when they are not; and happiness or misery are proportioned in him according to the degree of his gratification or disappointment. It follows that his liberty and happiness are the same thing. He would always be completely happy if he had always the power of executing his will, and the degree of his happiness is always proportionate to the degree of his power.

This remark explains why men, even without suspecting it, are all so passionately fond of liberty; for they could not be otherwise, since whenever there exists a desire, under whatever name it may appear, the possibility of accomplishing that desire is implied, and willed or wished; it is always the possession of a portion of power, or the removal of some constraint, which constitutes a certain portion of happiness. The exclamation . . . "O if I could!" comprehends the desire of accomplishing all our wishes; every wish would be gratified if we could effect it by willing it; all powerful, or what is the same thing, entire liberty, is inseparable from perfect happiness.

This remark conducts us farther, and explains to us why men have formed to themselves different ideas of liberty, according to their different ideas of happiness. They must always have attached the idea of liberty in an eminent degree, to the power of doing what they please, and of which satisfaction is the attribute. Montesquieu, in his second chapter, appears to be astonished that many people should entertain false ideas of liberty, making it consist in things foreign to their solid interests, or at least not essential thereto; but he should have first considered that men have often placed their happiness and satisfaction in the enjoyment of unimportant or even hurtful things: the first fault committed, the second follows as a consequence. A Russian in the time of Peter the Great, placed his greatest interest in his long beard, which was in fact of no use, or an incumbrance, or very ridiculous. The native of Poland was passionately attached to his *liberum veto*, which was the great source of affliction to his country. Both Russians and Poles would have deemed themselves subjected to the greatest tyranny, if obliged to part with either; and their subjection was certainly great, when they were deprived thereof, for their strongest desires were frustrated. Montesquieu answers himself by adding this remarkable phrases. . . . "In fine, every one has called that government free, which was the most conformable to his inclinations;" which is unquestionably true, it could not be otherwise, and each has so expressed himself reasonably, because every one is truly free when all his wishes are gratified, and we cannot be free in any other manner.

From this last observation flows many consequences; the first which presents itself is. . .that a nation should be considered truly free as long as it continues satisfied with its government, even if in its nature the government should be less conformable to the principles of liberty than another which displeases him. . . . The Athenians, in adopting. . .imperfect laws, were certainly ill advised; but they were very free; while in modern times a great part of France, in receiving their constitution of the year three, (1795) however free it might be in its form, were really slaves, since it was established in opposition to their will; hence we may conclude, that institutions can be ameliorated only in proportion to the increase of information among the people at large, and even those which are the best absolutely are not always so relatively; for the better they are, the more opposed to false ideas, and if they are disagreeable to too great a number, they cannot be maintained without using forcible means, after which there could be no more liberty, no more happiness, no more security; this may serve as an apology for many institutions bad in themselves, which may have been at one period well adapted to the circumstances in which they existed, but furnishes no argument for our preserving them when they are found to be pernicious. . .and it may also serve to explain the causes of failure of many good institutions, and will not prevent us from adopting them at a more favorable time.

The second consequence of the observation which we have made above is, that the government under which the greatest liberty is enjoyed, whatever may be its form, is that which governs the best, for in it the greatest number of people are the happiest; and when we are as happy as we can be, our desires are accomplished as much as possible. If the most despotic prince should administer public affairs in a perfect manner, we should enjoy the greatest possible happiness under his rule, which is the same thing as *liberty* It is not then the form of government in itself, that is so important; it would indeed be a very weak argument in its favor, that it was in form more agreeable to reason, because it is not mere speculation or theory, which constitute the happiness of mankind in society, but practical good and beneficial results; for it concerns individuals who possess the faculties of life, and are sensible of good and evil, not ideal or abstract beings. Those, who in the political convulsions of our times, said. . ."I do not care about being free, all I desire is to be happy," uttered a sentiment contradictory in itself. . . .being both very sensible and very insignificant: sensible, in as much as happiness is the only object worthy of our attention; insignificant, in as much as happiness is really true liberty. For the same reason, those enthusiasts, who said that happiness is not to be taken into consideration, when liberty is in question, are guilty of the same absurdity; for if happiness could be separated from liberty, it should without hesitation be preferred: but we are not happy when we are not free, for certainly suffering is not doing as we wish. The only circumstance, therefore, which renders any one social organization preferable to another, is its being better adapted to render the members of society happy; and if in general it be desired, that the social constitution should leave to the people a great facility to make known their wishes, it is then more probable that under a government which secures this power, they are governed as they desire.

Let us examine, with Montesquieu, which are the principal conditions to be fulfilled in order to accomplish this end; and like him, let us only occupy ourselves on the question generally, without respect to any local or particular conjuncture.

This justly celebrated philosopher has remarked, in the first place, that public functions may be reduced to three principles: that of making laws. . .that of conducting internal and external affairs, according to the intention of the laws. . . . and, that of passing judgment on private or civil differences, as well as on accusations of private and public offences: that is to say, in other words. . .that social action is comprised in *willing, executing,* and *judging.*

Then it may be easily perceived that these three great functions, or even two of them, could not be united in the same person or persons, without the greatest danger to the rest of the citizens; for if the same man, or body of men, were at the same time authorised to will and to execute, the single person or the body of men, would be too powerful for any to interpose or form a judgment, and consequently would be obliged to submit. If the one only who made the law also judged, it is probable that he would soon rule the one entrusted with the execution of the law; and in short, this last person who executes, being always the most to be feared, on account of the physical force entrusted to him; if he should be invested with the function of judging, there can be no doubt that he would soon so arrange the means of authority, that the legislating power must enact such laws as he should please.

These dangers are too palpable to attach any merit to their discovery; the great difficulty appears to be, how to devise the means of avoiding them. Montesquieu spares himself the trouble of such an enquiry, by persuading himself that they are already found. . . . He is so well satisfied of the problem being solved, that he says in another phace. . . "To discover political liberty in the constitution, does not require so much trouble, if we can possess it where it is; if we have found it, why seek it:" and he immediately presents the form of the English government, as he imagined it to exist in its administration. It is true, that at the period in which he wrote, England was a very flourishing and celebrated state; its government was, of those till then known, that which produced, or appeared to produce, the most flattering results in every respect. However, this superiority, partly real, partly apparent, but in a greater measure the effect of causes wholly foreign, should not have prepossessed so strong a mind as Montesquieu, or induced him to suppress the errors of the theory, or to insinuate that it leaves nothing more to be desired.

This prepossession in favor of English institutions and ideas, led him in the first place to forget, that the legislative, executive, and judicial functions, are properly only delegated trusts, functions which may indeed confer power and credit, on the persons invested with them, but are not therefore self-existent in the persons who exercise them. There is by *right*, only one power in society, and that is the will of the nation or society, from which all authority flows; and in fact there is not any other change, than that of the authority delegated to the man, or body of men, of the several functions by which they disburse the necessary expences, and exercise all the physical force of the society. Montesquieu does not deny this, he is only unmindful of it; he is entirely taken up with his triple powers, his legislative, executive, and judiciary, considering them as rivals, and as powers independent of each other; and that it is only necessary to reconcile or restrain them, each by the other, in order to make every thing go on well, without taking any notice, whatever, of the natural power from which they are derived, and upon which they depend.

By not perceiving that his executive power is the only real one in fact, and that it influences all the others, he concedes, without consideration or enquiry, this power to an individual, and even makes it hereditary in that individual's family, and for no other reason than because one man is better calculated for action than many: if this principle were well founded, it would have been yet worth enquiry, whether if an individual be so much better fitted for action, he would suffer any other free action to exist round him; and moreover, whether this individual, chosen at hazard, is so likely to be competent to the exercise of that wise deliberation which should precede every action.

He also approves of the legislative power, being confided to the legislators, freely elected by the people for a limited period, and from all parts of the nation; but what is still more extraordinary, he approves of the existence of the privileged hereditary body in the nation, and that this body should compose of itself, by right, a part of the legislative body, distinct and separate from that elected by the people, and that it should possess the right of a negative upon the resolves of the elected representatives! His reasons are curious; it is, he says, "because their prerogatives are *odious in themselves,* and they should be enabled to defend them;" it would seem a more natural conclusion, we should think, that being odious they should rather be abolished.

He also thinks, that this second section of the legislative body is very useful, because there can be placed therein, all that is really important in the judiciary authority, the passing of judgment on crimes against the state; so that, as he says, it becomes the *regulating power,* of which both the executive and legislative powers stand in need to mutually temper them. He does not look to facts in the history of England, nor perceive what it attests, that the house of lords is any thing else, rather than an independent and regulating power; that it is in fact, only an appendage to the court, the advanced guard of the executive power, whose fortunes it has always followed; and that giving this irresponsible body a negative in legislation and a high judiciary function, is only investing the court with an additional force, and rendering the punishment of state criminals a matter of mere discretion with the executive, or rendering it impossible to punish whenever it is not the pleasure of the court.

Notwithstanding these advantages, and the great power which the executive has at its disposal, he does not think the right of a negative upon the laws necessary to the executive; nor that of convoking, nor of proroguing, nor of dissolving them; and he imagines that the popular representatives possess a sufficient defence, in their precautionary power of voting the supplies only for one year, as if they must not renew them every year, or witness a dissolution of the government; and that this power is further augmented by their having it in their discretion to prohibit or permit the raising of a military force, or the establishment of camps, barracks, or fortified places; as if they must not be forced into the establishment of either, whenever a necessity shall call for it. . . .a necessity which the executive can at any time create.

Montesquieu terminates this long detail, by a sentence obscure and embarrassed. . . . "This is the fundamental constitution of the government of which we speak; the legislative body being composed of two parts, each of them constrains the other, by their mutual preventative faculty; both are restrained by the executive which will itself be restrained by the legislative;" and to this he adds this singular reflection: "These three powers should naturally form a state of repose or inaction; but as in the nature of things they must move, they are under the necessity of acting in concert." I must acknowledge, that I do not perceive the absolute necessity of this conclusion; on the contrary, it appears evident, that where every thing is constituted, so as to constrain or impede motion, nothing can be perfectly accomplished. If the king were not effectively master of the parliament, and if he did not consequently lead them, I can see nothing in this weak fabric of government that could prevent him; neither can I perceive any thing in favor of such an organization. . .which is in my opinion very imperfect. . . but a circumstance which belongs to it rather than forming a part of it, and which has not been noticed. . .that is, the constancy with which the nation wills that it should so subsist. But as at the same time, they are wisely attached to the maintenance of personal liberty and the freedom of the press, the power is always preserved of making the public opinion known; so that when the king abuses his power, of which he really possesses too much, he is subject to be opposed by a general movement in favor of those who resist his oppression; as has been twice exemplified in the seventeenth century, and which is always very easy in an island, where there can be no motives, consistent with the principles of the government, for maintaining a large standing army. This is in fact the only effective veto, which is to be found under the English constitution, compared with which all the rest are nothing.

The great point in the English constitution is, that the nation six or seven times deposed its kings: but then it must be remarked, that this is not a constitutional expedient; it is rather an insurrection arising out of necessity, as it was formerly said to be according to the laws of Crete. Legislative deposition, to my great astonishment, Montesquieu praises in another part of his book, notwithstanding it is certain that this remedy is so cruel, that a sensible people would endure great evils, before they could resort to it; and though it may happen that they defer redress so long, that if the usurpation be conducted with address, the people may insensibly acquire the habit of slavery so inveterately, as no longer to feel the desire, or may cease to possess the capacity, of breaking their chains by any means.

What very much characterises the warmth of Montesquieu's imagination, is, that on the faith of three lines from Tacitus, which would require a compendious commentary, he has persuaded himself, that he found among the savages of ancient Germany, the model and the spirit of the government, which he considers as a masterpiece of human reason; in the excess of his admiration, he thus exclaims. . ."This excellent system was discovered in the woods:" and a little after he adds. . ."It does not belong to me to examine whether the English actually enjoy liberty or not, it is sufficient to say, it is established by their laws." Nevertheless, I am of opinion, that the first point was well worthy of examination, were it only to assure himself, that he had a just knowledge of the second; because if he had bestowed more attention on *their laws,* he would have discovered that among the English, there exists really no more than *two* powers instead of three; that these two powers exist only when both are present, because one has all the real force and no public attachment, while the other possesses no force, but enjoys all the public confidence, until it manifests a disposition to overpower its rival, and sometimes even then: that these two powers, by uniting, are legally competent to the change of the public established laws, and even those which determine their relations and their existence, for no law obstructs them, and they have exercised this power on various occasions: so that, in fact, liberty is not truly established by their political laws; and if the English really enjoy liberty to a certain extent, it originates in the causes which I have explained, and has reference to certain received usages in their civil and criminal proceedings, rather than to positive laws; as, in fact, it is altogether without law established.

The great problem, therefore, of the distribution of the powers of society, so that neither of them may trespass on the authority of the other, or the limits assigned them by the general interests; and that it may always be easy to keep them within bounds, or to bring them back by peaceable and legal means, is not, I conceive, resolved in that country: I would rather claim this honor for the United States of America, the constitution of which determines what should be done when the executive, or when the legislative, or when both together, go beyond their legitimate powers, or are in opposition to each other; and when it becomes necessary to change the constitutional act of a state, or of the confederation itself.

5 *Pierre-Claude-Francois Daunou*

Pierre-Claude-Francois Daunou (1761-1840) was associated with the school of Ideology but differed from its founder, Destutt de Tracy, in that his primary interests were political and in that his specific effort was to free liberalism from any need to rely on what he regarded as metaphysical assumptions as the Declaration of the Rights of Man of 1790 had done. Instead, recalling Jeremy Bentham, Daunou tried to argue empirically, to determine what means were best suited in practice to secure certain ends. Moreover, it is clear that Daunou was writing in the context of a particular historical situation, the Restoration.

The word garanties *is sometimes translated here as "safeguards" rather than "guarantees."*

The system to be developed in this essay is the following: to show on the one hand that the security of persons and property and the freedom of industry, opinions, and conscience are the only individual interests that are also rights, and that any further claims are useless, unwise, or unjust demands; and to show on the other hand that all governments, regardless of their names and their ways of operation, can provide substantive and sufficient safeguards provided that they sincerely allow the representatives of the nation to participate in the formulation of laws, and provide for the independence of judges and the functioning of juries. By the word "government" I refer to the supreme power, charged not only with executing the laws but also with proposing and promulgating them, with attending to the suppression of offenses and crimes and the execution of sentences.

Therefore, although the purpose of this essay is to claim a guarantee of all the rights subsumed under the word "liberty," it also has the effect, no less directly, of reaffirming and further

SOURCE. P.-C.-F. Daunou, *Essai sur les garanties individuelles que reclame l'etat actuel de la societe,* 3rd revised ed., Paris: 1822, pp. ii-iv, 3-8, 263-5.

developing legitimate power: it excludes only despotism, usurpation, and tyranny. As applied to contemporary France it demands nothing beyond what is contained in the Charter [of 1814], it even stops short of some of its undertakings; and if it conflicts with certain laws passed since 1814 this is because those undertaking condemned them in advance.

Some very enlightened men maintain that opposition is a necessary element in a representative system. This is a theory which I shall try to refute; but I shall also attempt to prove that the idea of allowing the ministers and the two Chambers the power to modify the constitution is subversive of any social guarantee. These and certain other similar theories have come to us from England which, except for the jury and freedom of the press (which we have not taken from England), has not for a long time, certainly not since 1814, had any model of a public institution to offer us which was preferable or even comparable to our own. . . .

The safeguards [enumerated above] are just about the only limits which, in a great state, can usefully circumscribe authority. . . . A society that succeeds in protecting all its inhabitants from oppression will by that very fact be so peaceful that the rulers can well be entrusted with the task of making it happier. . . .

Even when reduced to such simple terms the problem nevertheless still presents serious difficulties, all stemming from the fact that in certain circumstances the public power is obliged to use coercion on persons or on property, to prohibit or require certain actions. In fact, it can prevent crimes only by seizing those who are about to attempt them; it maintains order only by spending funds to which everyone must contribute; and in order to maintain social relations it is sometimes obliged to enforce their respect. What is to be prevented is that the public power should become aggressive under the guise of paternalism. To be sure, the line between these two kinds of actions is sometimes so thin that the government itself may make a mistake.

In such matters, general ideas become reliable only to the extent that they result from an examination of a large enough number of particular instances. We shall therefore investigate successively in what the security of persons, the security of property, and the freedom of industry, opinions, and conscience consist; by what

aggressive acts the public power can violate them; and what rules
and what institutions can protect us from its excesses. Considering
various governments from this point of view alone we shall divide
them into only two classes, according to whether they accord or
refuse these safeguards, unless, in order to include all the facts and
to make the enumeration complete, we should be obliged to form a
third category of those governments which promise the safeguards
but make them illusory by means of exceptional laws in particular
circumstances. . . .

I shall nowhere need to have recourse to abstract principles, to
the origins of sovereign power, to the hypothesis of a social
contract. . . . I take as my point of departure a single *datum*
derived from languages, the depositaries of the ideas and feelings
of the civilized human race. I shall not go beyond the words that
express the desire to be protected from the attacks of public power
as well as of private persons. . . .

I believe that all the true interests of the governed are included
in what I have called individual guarantees. I know that this is
not enough for the ambitious, who want not merely guarantees
but jobs, honors, power; and I know also that such an irregular
state of affairs is common in troubled times, not only because it is
one of the results of an overthrow of all the elements of social order
but also because in such times power, though more dangerous
than ever, is regarded as a guarantee and in fact the only possible
one. But the disorder, as it continues, dispels these illusions; and
when it clears away people understand better than before that
personal liberty, security of the home, the development of private
industry, and independence in running one's personal affairs are
the only real interests there are and that nothing is to be asked of
the government save that it guarantee them. I am persuaded that
it can suit nobody, either before or after revolutions, to be liable to
illegal arrest, indefinite detention, inequitable justice, arbitrary
prohibitions, expropriations, violence, *coups d'etat,* or exile. . . .

What danger or harm, in fact, do these guarantees threaten to
those who hold power? What is it, after all, that these guarantees
ask?

That none may be arrested or detained without being tried
according to ordinary rules of justice with the least possible delay;

That legally held property be inviolable and not subject to arbitrary extortion;

That industry, even if not freed from all impediments, should at least not have to fear a return of those that already been abolished;

That insult, slander, and sedition be treated as offenses or crimes; and that all other opinions expressed orally or in writing or in the press be free from all censorship, whether prior or subsequent, and from all administrative directives;

That the religion privileged by the state [that is, the Roman Catholic], financially supported by all citizens including those who do not profess it, should in no way or respect restrict the freedom of any other religious belief;

These are .the only points to be guaranteed, and the only institutions strictly necessary to accomplish this are the following:

That all judges. . ;be permanent, not subject to transfer or displacement against their will, and irremovable except by reason of duly pronounced dereliction of duty;

That all matters to be punished as crimes or other offenses be verified and declared as such previously by juries whose selection does not rest with the supreme authority or its agents and may not be influenced by the presidents of courts or tribunals;

Finally, that an assembly of representatives regularly and freely elected. . .without ministerial influence shall in entire independence express its assent to all taxes, loans, and new laws.

It is to be noted that such limitations in fact defend the supreme power even more than they inhibit it. For what do they forbid it to commit except frauds, crimes, and misdeeds like those which it puts down? It is these limitations that distinguish legitimate power from tyrannical or usurped force; the latter enjoys security only by keeping a people supersititious and degraded, in darkness and misery; legitimate power, by contrast, itself profits from the guarantees that it gives, the lights that it allows to shine around it, the industries that it stimulates, the property that it protects and respects. . . .

Germaine de Stael (1766-1817), daughter of Louis XVI's finance minister Necker, though far more of a literary than a strictly political writer, became like the Ideologues persona non grata *with Napoleon and went abroad. From her exile, and after Napoleon's overthrow, she became notable for introducing into France from Germany the specifically Romantic connection between literary and political ideas, and she may legitimately be regarded as the founder of the classical tradition of French liberalism in the first half of the nineteenth century. She exerted her influence particularly through her lover and disciple Benjamin Constant (see below).*

The following extracts are taken from a variety of Mme. de Stael's writings.

[1799] In France people will always believe that things will go better if the government does not act. Far from calling for its assistance, people regard it as an obstacle. The social order being much better organized than in the past, agriculture and commerce being easier to manage, the government—that is, the common power—is no longer necessary to each person. Since private life easily provides many pleasures, the government is no longer called upon to serve people's personal concerns. One must start from this great difference, in order to base the Republic in France upon a very small number of personal sacrifices. It must also be borne in mind that the political unit among the ancients was very small; practically all men taking part in public affairs felt compensated for their trouble by rewards or the hope of rewards. But in France, where seven hundred men out of twenty-five million are called upon to deal with public affairs, the odds against ambition are too

SOURCE. *Madame de Stael on Politics, Literature and National Character,* translated by Morroe Berger, pp. 93-94, 104, 114-5, 120-1, 137-141, 213-7, 226-230. Copyright c 1964 by Morroe Berger: Reprinted by permission of Doubleday & Company, Inc. and Sidgwick & Jackson Ltd. The extracts are arranged chronologically rather than in the order in which they appear in Berger's edition.

great to make it worth the bother. Such a government, though free and derived from the principle of popular sovereignty, must, like monarchies, be careful not to disturb the tranquillity of the mass of citizens. Civil liberty and individual liberty must be highly respected in a country where all men cannot be granted the effective and varying exercise of political liberty.

To win over public opinion, then, the ancients had to move the soul, to stir up patriotism through conquests, triumphs, and dissension and even disorders, which brought all the emotions into play. In France we must no doubt shape a national spirit to the extent that we can. But we must not lose sight of the fact that public opinion will be based upon the love of tranquillity, the desire to acquire wealth, and the need to preserve it; that people will always be more concerned with administrative concepts than political questions because they bear more directly upon private life; and that, while keeping in mind the lofty goal of elevating the French nation to the level of all philosophical ideas and all republican institutions, every individual's private sphere must always be respected.

Rome's well-being embraced the well-being of all Roman citizens, and invariably generated enthusiasm by proposing the sacrifice of personal interests to the common good—not that the Romans were more generous than we are, but because the contribution of each individual was outweighed by the benefit he derived from the common weal. But in France, where the situation is reversed, the only thing that can make people prefer the Republic is respect for private life and private wealth. In the present era liberty means everything that protects citizens' independence of the government. The liberty of ancient times means everything that ensured citizens the largest share in the exercise of power. These two great differences make it necessary that the Republic in France not demand things of or exert pressure upon the people, that it be guided by a preventive ethic rather than a doctrine of sacrifice that becomes brutal when it ceases to be voluntary—in short, we must remember that progress in the technique of social organization, having made private welfare easier to achieve, has alienated citizens all the more from sacrificing for the common good. For public opinion, so placid, so submissive to the slightest demonstration of force, is at the same time the only invincible power. It cannot be conquered, for it does not fight. Its influence cannot be destroyed, for it is the influence of each and of all. It cannot be made to change its mind, for it wants only its well-being. So long as there is war its existence may be ignored, but since it is the true national power, as soon as we want to base government upon realities we must rally public opinion to the Republic—or the government will not firmly establish itself.

[1800] Liberty, virtue, honor, knowledge: an imposing procession of man in his natural dignity—these related ideas of the same origin could not exist separately. The fulfillment of each lies in the union of all.

The advancement of literature, that is to say, the perfection of the art of thinking and of expressing one's self, is essential to the establishment and preservation of freedom. It is obvious that knowledge becomes the more indispensable in a country as all its citizens have a direct part in the conduct of government. And it is equally true that political equality, the principle inherent in every structure based upon reason, cannot endure unless degree of education as the criterion for classifying people is followed with even more care than feudalism exercised in its arbitrary distinctions. Purity of language and nobility of expression—manifestations of the elevation of the soul—are necessary above all in a state founded upon a democratic basis. In others, artifical barriers make the external signs of good education irrelevant; but when power rests only on the supposition of personal worth, what care ought not to be taken to maintain for such merit all of its external signs?

In a democratic state there is always the fear that the desire for popularity may lead to imitation of vulgar taste; before long one could be persuaded that it is useless, and all but harmful, to have too marked a superiority to the crowd one wants to master. The people would accustom themselves to choosing ignorant and stupid rulers, these rulers would extinguish all enlightenment, and by an inevitable route the loss of enlightenment would bring back the enslavement of the people.

In a free state it is impossible for public authority to do without the genuine consent of the citizens it governs. Reason and eloquence are the natural ties of a republican society. What power can one have over the free will of men without this force, this sincerity, of language that reaches people and inspires them with its message? When one does not know how to convince, one oppresses; in all power relations among governors and governed, as ability declines, usurpation increases.

New institutions must create a new spirit in countries that people want to make free. But how can anything be based upon public opinion without the help of distinguished writers? The desire to obey rather than to command obedience must be aroused; and even though a government rightly wishes the establishment of such institutions it must be solicitous enough of public opinion to seem to be only granting its wish. Only sound writings can in the long run direct and change certain national habits. In the privacy of his thought, man has an asylum of liberty that violence cannot penetrate; indeed, conquerors have often taken over the customs of the conquered: conviction alone has changed long-standing customs. It is through the advancement of literature that we can successfully combat old prejudices. Governments in countries that have just become free must, in order to destroy old errors, use ridicule, which will set the youth against these errors, and conviction, which will alienate the mature. Such governments must, in order to lay the foundation of new institutions, arouse interest, hope, enthusiasm, in short those creative sentiments that give birth to everything that exists, to everything that endures; and it is in the art of the spoken and written word that we find the only means to inspire such sentiments.

Among the various achievements of the human mind, it is philosophical literature—eloquence and reason—that I regard as the true guarantee of liberty. The sciences and the arts are a very important part of intellectual activity; but their discoveries, their successes, exercise no direct influence upon that public opinion that decides the destiny of nations. Geometricians, physicists, painters, and poets may well receive encouragement under the reign of almighty kings, whereas to such masters political and religious inquiry may appear to be the most dangerous kind of rebellion.

Those who devote themselves to the study of the exact sciences, never running into the emotions of men, become accustomed to considering only what is susceptible to mathematical proof. These scholars almost always classify as an illusion whatever they cannot submit to the logic of calculation. They assess first the strength of the government, whatever its form; and as they have no other wish than to devote themselves quietly to their work, they are inclined to obedience to the ruling authority. The profound thought required by abstraction in the exact sciences diverts the scholars from concerning themselves with the affairs of life; and nothing pleases absolute monarchs more than men so deeply occupied with the physical laws of the world that they leave the human realm to whoever is determined to take it. Undoubtedly the discoveries of science must in the long run give a new strength to that higher philosophy that judges of nations and kings; but so remote a future does not in the least intimidate tyrants; we have seen many of them patronizing the sciences and arts, but all of them fear those natural enemies of patronage itself, the thinkers and the philosophers.

Poetry, of all the arts, is the one that is closest to reason. Yet poetry does not allow the kind of analysis or inquiry that is useful in the discovery and propagation of knowledge of philosophical ideas. Anyone who would like to enunciate a new and bold truth would prefer to write in language that conveys thought exactly and precisely; he would seek to persuade by reasoning rather than to carry away by imagination. Poetry has more often been dedicated to the praise of despotic power than to its censure. The fine arts in general can sometimes contribute, by their very pleasures, to molding subjects as tyrants wish them. The arts can, by the amusements of each day, divert the mind from any grand and commanding conception; they lead men back to their feelings, and they instill in the mind a sensuous outlook, a deliberate indifference, a passion for the present and a neglect of the future, all highly favorable to tyranny. In a curious contrast, the arts, which enable us to enjoy life, make us rather indifferent to death. Only deep emotion, creating a passionate will to reach their objective, bind us firmly to life; but a life devoted to pleasures amuses without persuading; it prepares us for intoxication, sleep, and death. During eras famous for their sanguinary repressions, the Romans and the French devoted themselves to public amusements with the greatest eagerness, whereas in contented republics, family attachments, sober pursuits, the love of fame and reputation, often turn people away from even the delights of the fine arts. The only literary force that can make unjust rulers tremble is noble expression, independent inquiry, which judges in the court of reason all the institutions and all the beliefs of mankind.

It was often said during the Revolution in France that a certain amount of despotism was necessary to establish liberty. This is a contradiction in terms that has been made into a maxim, but it changes nothing in the reality of things. Institutions based upon force may simulate everything about liberty, except its genuine workings; they may be so much like their models in form as to startle you by the resemblance: you will recognize everything in them—except life.

People are rather generally convinced that the republican spirit calls for a change in the character of literature. I consider this notion correct but in a different sense from that given it. The republican spirit calls for more rigor in good taste, which is inseparable from good manners. It also undoubtedly permits literature to convey a more forceful kind of beauty, a more philosophical and more moving portrait of the great events of life. . . . Since a republic necessarily brings forth stronger emotions, the art of portrayal must grow as its subjects grow. But by an odd contrast, it is largely the licentious and the shallow *genre* that has sought to take advantage of the liberty that literature was believed to have acquired.

The precepts of taste as they apply to republican literature are more simple but no less rigorous than those adopted by the writers of the age of Louis XIV. Under the monarchy, convention was sometimes substituted for reason and propriety for true feelings. But since in a republic taste should consist only in perfect understanding of all true and enduring relations, to lack the elements of taste is to be unaware of the real nature of things.

Under the monarchy, it was often necessary to disguise bold condemnation, to veil a new opinion under the form of received prejudices. The taste that had to be brought to these various appearances required an unusually delicate *finesse.* But the guise of truth, in a free country, is in harmony with truth itself. Expression and feeling ought to spring from the same source.

Formerly, people combined nobility of manners with an almost habitual practice of jesting. This combination presupposes a perfection of taste and refinement, a sense of one's superiority, power, and status which education for equality does not develop.

This elegance, grand and trivial at the same time, probably does not suit republican manners; it is too distinctively characteristic of the practices of great wealth and high status. Intellect is more democratic; it waxes at random among all men independent enough to have some leisure. It is intellect, therefore, that we must encourage above all in literature, by devoting ourselves less to subjects that depend exclusively upon formal elegance.

Politeness is the tie society has established between strangers. Certain qualities attach us to family, friends, and the unfortunate. But in all those relations that have not yet assumed the character of a duty, civility of manners anticipates sympathy, moderates firm beliefs, and maintains for every one the place in the world that his merit ought to bring him. It marks the degree of respect to which each person has raised himself; in this sense, it distributes the rewards that are the goal of life's labors. . . .

Under the monarchy, the spirit of chivalry, the ceremony of rank, the magnificence of wealth—everything that strikes the imagination— compensated in some respects for the lack of true merit. But in a republic women no longer count for anything if they do not inspire respect everywhere by their natural nobility. As soon as an illusion is banished, a reality must be substituted. As soon as an ancient prejudice is destroyed, a new virtue is needed. So a republic, far from having to afford greater liberty in customary social relations, must protect itself much more scrupulously against all kinds of lapses from propriety; for all distinctions in it are based only on personal qualities. If a reputation is in the slightest injured it is no longer possible, as in a monarchy, for a man to improve his position by his rank, birth, or any privilege extraneous to his own merit.

It is essential in France to establish ties that can reconcile opposing groups, and civility is an effective means to achieve this goal. It would unite all enlightened men, who would constitute a court of opinion which would dispense blame or praise with some justice.

This court would also exert an influence upon literature. Writers would know where to rediscover national taste and intellect, and would labor to portray and enlarge it.

Civility alone can soften the asperities of the partisan spirit. It permits mutual toleration long before affection, and intercourse long before agreement. And so our profound aversion for those we did not know is gradually weakened by conversation, consideration, and solicitude, which kindles sympathy and leads us ultimately to find fellow men among those we formerly regarded as enemies. . . .

It is only in free states that the genius for action and the genius for reflection can be united. In the Old Regime it was desirable that literary talent should almost always imply the absence of political talent.

In absolute monarchies people want a kind of mystery to suffuse the qualities suited to government so that an influential and barren mediocrity may push aside a superior intellect.

Great talent is no doubt necessary in order to govern well. But it was only in order to brush aside talent that people tried to argue that the reflection that creates the profound philosopher, the great writer, and the eloquent orator has no connection with the rules that should guide the leaders of nations. . . .

For the happiness of mankind, the great men charged with its destiny must have a certain number of very different qualities in almost equal degrees. A single type of superiority is not enough to win over the various forms of opinion and worth, nor does it, if I may put it so, adequately personify the conception we like to develop of a man of renown.

But, it may be said, what ought to be feared above all in a republic is enthusiasm for one man.

Nothing is less philosophical—that is to say, nothing would lead less to happiness—than the jealous narrowmindedness that would deprive nations of their place in history by equalizing the reputations of men. Every effort should be made to spread general education. But along with this great concern for the promotion of knowledge we must allow the goal of individual glory. A republic must give much more scope to this motive of emulation than any other form of government, for it grows richer with the manifold labors emulation inspires. Only a small number of men succeed, but all may aspire. And if fame crowns only success, the effort itself often has some hidden use.

The guiding principle of a republic in which political equality is sacred ought to be the establishment of the most pronounced distinctions among men in accordance with their talents and qualities.

Conquerors fear the soldiers who have helped them conquer

their empire, priests fear the very fanaticism on which all their power depends, and the ambitious mistrust their own devices—but enlightened men who reach the highest rank in the state do not cease to love and to disseminate knowledge. Reason has nothing to fear from reason, and philosophic minds base their strength upon their peers.

It would undoubtedly be difficult to subject human affairs to measurement, even to the calculus of probability. In the exact sciences all the foundations are unchanging, but in human matters everything depends upon circumstances. Things can be settled only by a multitude of considerations, some of which are so ephemeral that they often elude even expression—and measurement all the more. Condorcet, nevertheless, in his work on probability, has shown clearly how we might know in advance, almost with certainty, the opinion of a group on any subject. Applied to a large number of cases, the calculus of probability yields a virtually infallible result. Gamblers use it as a guide, however much their goal may seem to be subject to the whims of chance. It may likewise be applicable to the multitude of events making up the political sciences.

Mortality and birth tables present results that are certain and invariable, as long as the regular order of events continues. The number of divorces that will take place annually, the number of thefts and murders that will be committed in a country of a given population and religious and political condition—such numbers can be calculated precisely. So the events that depend upon the daily concurrence of all the human emotions occur as regularly and punctually as those subject only to the physical laws of nature. . . . If this is so, is it not then possible to show that the affairs of the human order are as regular as those of the physical order, and to base exact predictions upon these known events?

These predictions must be based upon the unchanging uniformity of a mass and not upon the diversity of individual units. Individually, all units of the human order are different. But if you take a hundred thousand persons at random you can make a fair approximation of the proportion who are enlightened, weak, wicked, and intellectually superior. You can determine this even more precisely if you introduce into the calculation the influence of the interest of class, that is, as in physics, the momentum that a certain slope or inclination gives to movement. By adding to this calculation the tested knowledge of the effects of this or that institution, one could base governmental functions upon almost certain foundations, measure the resistance one could expect to meet, and balance these functions among themselves in accordance with their real operation and the force of the obstacles to this operation.

Why should we not one day succeed in drawing up tables that would contain the solution of every political issue in accordance with statistical information and precise data collected on every country? One might then say the following: If we want to govern a particular people, we must require such and such a sacrifice of individual liberty—consequently, certain laws and a certain regime are appropriate to that realm. Or: For a country of a particular wealth and size, such and such a degree of force is necessary in the executive power—consequently, a certain degree of authority would be proper in one region though regarded as tyrannical in another. Such and such an equilibrium is necessary in order to establish a proper balance among governmental power—consequently, one constitution might be inapplicable and another might be necessarily despotic. . . .

Politics is a science yet to be created. One can as yet make out only vaguely the combination of experiment and principles that will lead to such precise results that all the problems of the human sciences may be successfully subjected, so to speak, to mathematical sequence, inference, and proof. The elements of the science are not fixed. What we call general ideas are only particular facts.

In America many political problems seem to be solved, for the citizens there are happy and free. But this good fortune depends upon special circumstances and so offers no guide to anything, neither the invariable rules themselves nor their applicability in another country.

Even less may we offer as a proof of the progress of the human mind in politics the long duration and almost indestructible stability of some governments in Europe, which, maintaining themselves by their power and keeping domestic peace and tranquillity, secure to mankind some benefits of association. Despotism dispenses with political science, just as force dispenses with knowledge and authority makes persuasion unnecessary. But these methods cannot be admitted to the discussion of mankind's interests. Force is an affair of chance, destructive of everything pertaining to thought and reasoning, the exercise of which always presupposes freedom.

In politics, then, the philosophers should set themselves the task of arranging the facts known to them in precise combinations, in order to draw sure results in accordance with the number and nature of the probabilities.

It is true that no calculation requires a larger number of different combinations. If a physical experiment can fail because a slight difference in the processes or a slight degree more or less of heat or cold has not been taken into account, what study of the human heart is not required in order to determine the degree of respect that ought to be given to government so that it may be obeyed, but without its power becoming unjust, and to determine the power legislators need to unite the nation in a single spirit, but without shackling individual genius! What a practiced glance is required to indicate the precise point where executive authority ceases to be a benefit and its absence an evil! There is no problem composed of a greater number of terms, and none in which error would have more dangerous consequences.

Philosophy today must rest upon two bases, morality and calculation. But there is one rule from which we must never depart: whenever the calculation does not agree with morality, the calculation is false, however incontestable its exactitude may appear at first glance.

It has been said that the French Revolution barbarous theorists took mathematical calculations as the basis of their bloody laws and coldly sacrificed the lives of several thousand individuals to what they regarded as the happiness of the greater number.

These atrocious men thought they could simplify their calculations by omitting suffering, feeling, and imagination; they had no conception of the nature of general truths. These truths are made up of every fact and every individual being. Calculation is neither good nor useful unless it recognizes all exceptions and regularizes all differences. If a single case is allowed to escape, the result will be false, just as the slightest numerical error makes the solution of a problem impossible.

Politics is subject to calculation because, applying always to men united in a mass, it is based upon a scheme that is general, and therefore abstract. But morality, whose purpose is the preservation of the rights and happiness of each person, is necessary to force politics to respect, in its combinations, the happiness of individuals. Morality must guide our calculations, and our calculations must guide politics. . . .

[1816] We cannot watch too attentively for the first symptoms of tyranny. . . . Despite differences of time and place, there are points of similarity in the history of all nations that have fallen under the yoke. It is almost always after prolonged civil disturbance that tyranny becomes established, because it offers to all the exhausted and fearful parties the hope of finding shelter in it. Bonaparte has said of himself, with reason, that he could play the instrument of power marvellously. His plan for achieving control over France rested upon three main bases: to gratify men's self-interest at the expense of their virtues, to deprave public opinion with sophisms, and to give the nation the goal of war instead of liberty.

General Bonaparte decreed a constitution in which there were no safeguards. Besides, he took great care to leave in existence the laws announced during the Revolution, in order to select from this detestable arsenal the weapon that suited him. The special commissions, deportations, exiles, the bondage of the press—these steps unfortunately taken in the name of liberty—were very useful to tyranny. To adopt them, he sometimes advanced reasons of state, sometimes the need of the times, sometimes the acts of his opponents, sometimes the need to maintain tranquillity. Such is the artillery of phrases that supports absolute power, for "emergencies" never end, and the more one seeks to repress by illegal measures the more one creates disaffected people who justify new injustices. The establishment of the rule of law is always put off till tomorrow. This is a vicious circle from which one cannot break out, for the public spirit that is awaited in order to permit liberty can come only from liberty itself.

7   Benjamin Constant de Rebecque

Benjamin Constant (1767-1830), although deriving many of his ideas from the seminal mind of Mme. de Stael and although, like her, interested in literature as well as politics, was the first to cast the political theory of French classical liberalism into systematic form. During Napoleon's "Hundred Days" in 1815 he drafted the Additional Act which was designed to liberalize the Napoleonic constitution, but after 1815 he became a leading member of the liberal party during the Restoration.

The following essay was written in 1818 as an addition to his Principes de politique *of 1815. In a preface Constant himself says that he is now able to express his ideas on liberty more boldly than in that work dating from his association with Napoleon. This is a closely reasoned argument by a man steeped in the problems of political theory as well as exposed to the difficulties of politics in practice; at the same time, for all its severe tone, its style betrays the literary artist.*

ON POPULAR SOVEREIGNTY AND ITS LIMITS

. . .In acknowledging the principle of popular sovereignty, that is to say, the supremacy of the general will over all particular wills, it is necessary to get very clear the nature and extent of this principle. Without a precise and exact definition, which I have nowhere yet found, the triumph of theory could become a calamity on application. The abstract recognition of popular sovereignty in no way increases the sum of the liberty of individuals; and if this sovereignty is allowed a latitude that it should not have, liberty may be lost despite this principle or even because of it.

The precaution recommended and to be followed is all the more indispensable for the fact that party leaders, however pure their intentions, are always reluctant to limit sovereignty. They regard

SOURCE. *Benjamin Constant, Cours de politique constitutionnelle ou collection des ouvrages publies sur le gouvernement representatif,* edited with an Introduction by Edouard Laboulaye, 2 vols., Paris: 1861, I, 273-285.

themselves as its heirs-presumptive and are concerned to preserve it for future use even while it is in the hands of their enemies. They distrust this or that kind of government, this or that class of governors; but if they are allowed to organize authority after their own fashion and to entrust it to agents of their choice they will try to extend it to its maximum.

Unlimited popular sovereignty creates. . .a degree of power in human society too great by definition, which is an evil no matter in whose hands it is placed. Whether it is entrusted to a single man, to several, or to all, it will be found equally an evil. . . . There are weights too heavy for human hands.

The error of those who, out of a genuine love of liberty, have given popular sovereignty unlimited power derives from the way in which their political ideas have been formed. They have seen in history a small number of men, or even a single one, in possession of immense power which did a great deal of harm; but their anger was directed against the possessors of the power and not the power itself. Instead of destroying it they thought only of displacing it. It was a scourge which they considered a conquest. They endowed all of society with it. From there it was bound to pass to the majority, from there into the hands of a few men, often into the hands of one man; it did as much harm as before, and the examples, the objections, the arguments, and the facts against all political institutions multiplied.

In a society founded on popular sovereignty it is certain that no individual, no class, may subject the rest to its particular will; but it is false to say that society as a whole exercises unlimited sovereignty over its members.

The totality of the citizenry is sovereign in the sense that no individual, party, or group may arrogate sovereignty to itself if it has not been delegated to it. But it does not follow that the totality of citizens, or those who are invested with sovereignty by it, may wilfully dispose of the lives of individuals. There is, on the contrary, a part of human life which of necessity remains individual and independent and which as of right remains outside the jurisdiction of society. Sovereignty exists only in a limited and relative way. The jurisdiction of this sovereignty stops at the point where the independence of individual life starts. If society crosses this border it becomes as culpable as the despot whose title rests only on the sword of destruction; society cannot exceed its

competence without usurpation, the majority cannot do so
without becoming a faction. The consent of the majority by no
means suffices in all cases to make its acts legitimate; there are
some acts that nothing can make legitimate. When any authority
commits acts of this sort it matters little from what source it claims
to derive; it matters little whether it is called an individual or a
nation; it might be the entire nation with the exception of the
citizen whom it oppresses, and the act would still not be legitimate.

Rousseau did not recognize this truth, and this error has turned
his *Social Contract,* so often invoked on behalf of liberty, into the
most terrible aid to all kinds of despotism. . . . Once granted that
the general will can do everything, the representatives of that
general will are the more to be feared the more they declare
themselves to be merely the docile instruments of this so-called
will, and the more they have at their disposal the force or the
means of persuasion necessary to ensure its manifestation in the
form that suits them. These people, by virtue of the unlimited
extent of social authority, legalize that which no tyrant would
dare to do in his own name. They demand the accumulation of
offices that they need from the owner of this authority, the people,
whose omnipotence operates only to justify their encroachments.
The most unjust laws, the most oppressive institutions, are
compulsory as expressions of the general will for, as Rousseau says,
individuals, being entirely dedicated to the benefit of the body
social, can have no will other than this general will. . . . We can
see the consequences of this system appearing at all periods of
history, but they unfolded themselves to their full frightening
extent during our revolution: they have inflicted on sacred
principles wounds that may be difficult to heal. The more popular
the government of France became, the deeper these wounds. It
would be easy to show by innumerable quotations that the crudest
sophistries of the most ardent apostles of the Terror were in their
most revolting consequences merely perfectly appropriate consequences of Rousseau's principles. . . .

Rousseau himself was afraid of these consequences. Stricken
with terror at the sight of the immensity of social power he had
just created he did not know into which hands to place this
monstrous power and found no protection against the danger
inseparable from such a sovereignty except an expedient which

made its exercise impossible. He declared that sovereignty could be neither transferred, nor delegated, nor represented. This was to declare in other words that it could not be exercised; it amounted in practice to destroying the principle he had just proclaimed.

But the advocates of despotism are freer in taking this same axiom as their point of departure, for it supports and favors them. The man who reduced despotism to a system with the greatest intelligence, Hobbes, was not slow to declare sovereignty to be unlimited and to deduce from this the legitimacy of absolute government by one man. Sovereignty, he said, is absolute. . . . The people could divest themselves of this absolute sovereignty in favor of a monarch, who then became its legitimate possessor.

It is clear that the absolute character that Hobbes attributes to the people's sovereignty is the basis of his entire system. . . . This word "absolute" makes liberty,. . .peace, and happiness impossible under any kind of institution. Popular government is nothing but a convulsive tyranny, monarchical government merely a more concentrated kind of despotism.

When sovereignty is not limited there is no means of protecting individuals from governments. It is no good trying to subject governments to the general will. They will always dictate this will, and all precautions become illusory. . . . No political organization can avert this danger. You can try a division of powers; but if the sum total of powers is unlimited the divided powers have only to form a coalition for despotism to be installed without remedy. What is important for us is not that our rights may not be violated by one power without the approval of another, but rather that such a violation be forbidden to all powers. . . . The important truth, the eternal principle to be established is that sovereignty is limited, and that there are desires that neither the people nor their delegates have the right to entertain.

No authority on earth is unlimited, neither the people's, nor that of the men who claim to be their representatives, nor that of kings whatever their title to rule, nor that of the law which, being nothing but the expression of the will of the people or the prince, according to the form of government, must be kept within the same bounds as the authority from which it emanates.

These boundaries are fixed by justice and by the rights of individuals. Not even the will of an entire people can make just that which is unjust. The representatives of a nation do not have

the right to do what the nation itself has not the right to do . . . .
God, if he intervenes in human affairs, endorses only justice. The
right of conquest is merely force, which is not a right since it
passes to whoever seizes it. The consent of a people cannot make
legitimate what is illegitimate, since a people can delegate to
nobody an authority it does not have.

One objection presents itself to the limitation of sovereignty. Is
it possible to limit it? Is there a force that can prevent it from
breaking through the barriers prescribed for it? It will be said that
by ingenious devices power can be restrained by dividing it. Its
various parts can be placed in opposition and in equilibrium. But
by what means can the sum total be prevented from being
limitless? How can power be reined in other than by power?

Undoubtedly limitation of power in the abstract is not sufficient. We must look for the foundations of political institutions
which will so combine the interests of the various guardians of
power that their most obvious, most lasting, and most assured
advantage lies in each one of them remaining within the limits of
his respective functions. Nevertheless, the first problem remains the
competence and the limitation of sovereignty; for before we can
organize anything we must determine its nature and extent.

In the second place, without wishing, as philosophers have done
only too frequently, to exaggerate the influence of truth, we can
state that when certain principles are completely and clearly
demonstrated they serve in a sense as their own guarantees. A
universal opinion is formed concerning the evidence which soon
becomes victorious. It it is recognized that sovereignty is not
without limits, that is to say, that there is no unlimited power on
earth, then nobody will ever dare to claim such a power. This has
already been proved by experience. For example, society as a
whole is no longer given the right to put anyone to death without
trial. No modern government, therefore, claims to exercise such a
right. . . .

Limitation of sovereignty is therefore both genuine and possible.
It will be safeguarded, first of all by the force that safeguards all
truths recognized by public opinion, and second, more precisely,
by the distribution and balance of powers. . . . Everything else is
nothing but crude charlatanism, practised from century to century
for the benefit of some and to the misery and shame of the
rest. . . .

Contempt for thought is not a new discovery. . . . When false theories have misled men they readily listen to commonplace objections to theories, some from fatigue, some from self-interest, the great majority in imitation. But when they have recovered from their lassitude or escaped from their fears they recall that theory is not a bad thing in itself, that everything has a theory, that theory is nothing but practice reduced to rules by experience, and that practice is merely applied theory . . . . To declare that because false theories contain great dangers we must renounce all theories is to deprive men of the surest remedy against those very dangers; it amounts to saying that because error is fatal we must forever give up the search for truth. . . .

8   Victor Cousin

Victor Cousin (1792-1867) was by training a philosopher and in the early years of the Restoration started on a brilliant academic career. As the regime moved farther to the Right, however, Cousin's politics were considered dangerously liberal and, together with some others, he was removed from his academic post. Although his liberalism was in fact consciously moderate and eclectic he understandably became active in liberal opposition circles. When in 1828 he was reinstated in his Chair he at once became the idol of Parisian academic youth, whom he sought to teach and, indeed, inspire with liberal political notions founded in history as well as in philosophy. Later he was to serve the July Monarchy in various capacities as an educational administrator, being responsible, in particular, for the philosophy curriculum in French secondary schools for a generation. He also had profound literary interests which, like Constant's, are reflected in his style of argument and exposition that could hold a vast audience spellbound.

SOURCES. Victor Cousin, *History of Modern Philosophy,* translated by O. W. Wight, 2 vols., New York: 1893, I, 16-19, 25-28, 264, 268-271, 295-7; *Exposition of Eclecticism,* translated and edited by George Ripley, Edinburgh: 1839, in The Students' Cabinet Library of Useful Tracts, Vol. IV, Edinburgh: 1843, pp. 106-7, 132-3.

The first and longer series of extracts is taken from Cousin's lectures on the history of modern philosophy of 1828 to 1829 when he was at the height of his fame and popularity. Two short passages that follow are from the prefaces to the first and second editions respectively, in 1826 and 1833, of his Fragments philosophiques.

As soon as man has a consciousness of his being, he finds himself in a world strange and hostile, whose laws and phenomena seem in direct opposition to his own existence. For the purpose of self-defence he is endowed with intelligence and liberty. He defends himself, he lives, he breathes—though it be but two minutes in succession—only on condition of foreseeing, that is, on condition of having known these laws and these phenomena which would destroy his frail existence if he learned not little by little to observe them, to measure their influence, and to calculate upon their recurrence. By his intelligence he obtains knowledge of this world; by means of his liberty he modifies it, he changes it, he adapts it to his use; he arrests the spreading deserts, turns aside the rivers, and levels the mountains; in a word, he accomplishes in a succession of ages that series of prodigies which now so little astonishes us, because we are habituated to our power and to its effects. He who first measured the space which surrounded him, counted the objects which presented themselves to him, and observed their properties and their action, he it was who gave birth to the mathematical and physical sciences. He who modified in the least degree that which was an obstacle in his path, he it was who created industry. Multiply ages, cultivate this feeble plant by the accumulated labors of generations, and you will have all that you have to-day. The mathematical and physical sciences are a conquest of human intelligence over the secrets of nature. Industry is a conquest of liberty over the forces of this same nature. The world, such as man found it, was a stranger to him; the world, such as the mathematical and physical sciences, together with industry, have made it, is a world resembling man, reconstructed by him in his own image. In fact, look around you, and you will perceive everywhere the impression of intelligence and human liberty. Nature had only made things, that is, beings without value; man, in giving to them the form of his own personality, has elevated them into images of liberty and intelligence, and in this way communicated to them a part of the value which belongs to himself. The primitive world is nothing more than material for the labor of man; and it is labor that has given to this matter the value which it possesses. The destiny of man (I mean in his relations with the world) is to assimilate nature as much as possible to himself, to plant in it, and in it to make appear, unceasingly, the liberty and intelligence with which he is endowed. Industry, I repeat it with pleasure, is the triumph of man over nature, whose tendency was to encroach upon and destroy him, but which retreats before him, and is metamorphosed in his hands: this is truly nothing less than the creation of a new world by man. Political economy explains the secret, or rather the detail, of all this; it follows the achievements of industry, which are themselves connected with those of the mathematical and physical sciences.

I hope that I shall not be accused of injustice towards the mathematical and physical sciences, towards industry and political economy. I would simply demand whether there are no other sciences than mathematics and physics, whether there is no other power than that of industry, whether political economy exhausts all our intellectual capacity. Mathematics and physics, industry and political economy, have one and the same object, the useful. The question is then changed into this,—Is the useful the only want of our nature, the only idea upon which all the ideas of the understanding can be concentrated, the only view under which man considers all things, the only characteristic which he recognizes in them? No: it is a fact that, among all human actions, there are some that, besides their character of useful or hurtful, present still another, that of being just or unjust; a new character, indeed, but real and as certain as the first, and quite as worthy, too, of admiration.

The idea of the just is one of the glories of human nature. Man perceives it at first, but he perceives it only as a flash of lightning in the profound darkness of the primitive passions; he sees it continually violated by the disorder of passions and conflicting interests. That which he has been pleased to call a state of nature is only a state of war, where the right of the strongest rules, and where the idea of justice interposes only to be trampled under foot by passion. But at last this idea strikes also the mind of man, and it corresponds so well with what is most deeply planted within him, that little by little it becomes an imperious necessity of his nature to realize it; and, as before he had formed a new nature upon the idea of the useful, so now, in the place of primitive society, where all was confounded, he creates a new society on the basis of a new idea, that of justice. Justice constituted, is the State. The business of the State is to cause justice to be respected by force, upon the authority of this idea inherent in that of justice, viz., that injustice must not only be restrained, but punished. The State does not take into consideration the infinite variety of human elements that were at variance in the confusion and chaos of natural society. It does not embrace the whole man; it regards him only in his relation to the idea of the just and the unjust; that is, as capable of committing or receiving an injustice, or rather, as capable of being impeded or impeding others, either by fraud or violence, in the exercise of free and voluntary agency. Thence arise all duties and all legal rights. The only legal right is that of being respected in the peaceful exercise of liberty; the only duty, or at least the first of all, is to respect the liberty of others. Justice is nothing more than this; justice is the maintenance of reciprocal liberty. The State does not restrain liberty, as some aver, it develops and secures it. Besides, in primitive society, all men are necessarily unequal, by reason of their wants, their sentiments, their physical, intellectual, and moral faculties; but before the State, which considers men only as persons, as free beings, all men are equal, liberty being equal to itself, and forming the only type, the only measure of equality, which without liberty, is only a resemblance, that is, a diversity. Equality is then, with liberty, the basis of legal order and of this political world, a creation of the genius of man, more wonderful still than the actual world of industry compared with the primitive world of nature. . . .

Ideas, these are the proper objects of philosophy; in them philosophy has its world. Do not for a moment believe that ideas are the representatives of other things, and that it is on account of their resemblance with what they are destined to represent, that we give them credit. Ideas, as has been shown, represent nothing, absolutely nothing, except themselves. Ideas have but one character, viz., that of being intelligible: I add, that there is nothing intelligible but ideas; that they alone, often unknown to us, under such or such a form, gain our assent. Philosophy is the worship of ideas; it is the last victory of thought over every foreign form and element; it is the highest degree of liberty and intelligence.

Industry was already an enfranchisement from nature, the State a still greater one, art a new progress, religion a progress still more sublime; philosophy is the last enfranchisement, the last progress of thought.

Try, indeed, to derange the order in which I have successively presented to you the different spheres over which we have run: it is impossible for you to do it. Without industry, without security against the exterior world, without the State, without the subjection of the passions to the yoke of law, all regular exercise of thought is absolutely impossible. It cannot be that reflection preceded enthusiasm, and that philosophy went before, was anterior to art. The artist should not possess its secret; he becomes a philosopher only in ceasing to be an artist. It is the same with religion: in its holy images, in its august teachings, it contains every truth: not one is wanting; but all are there under a mysterious twilight. It is by faith that religion attaches itself to its objects; it is faith that it inspires; it is to faith that it addresses itself; it is this merit of faith that it wishes to obtain from humanity; and, in fact, it is a merit, it is a virtue in humanity to be able to believe what it sees not, in what it sees. But analysis and dialectics could not precede symbols and mysteries. The rational form is necessarily the last of all.

This form is also the most clear. Without doubt ideas are obscure to the senses, to the imagination, and to the soul: the senses see only the exterior objects upon which they fasten themselves; the imagination has need of representations, the soul of sentiments. Evidence is in the reason only. Philosophy is then the light of all lights, the authority of all authorities. Those who wish to impose upon philosophy and upon thought a foreign authority, do not think that of two things one must be true: either thought does not comprehend this authority, and then this authority is for it as if it were not; or it does comprehend it, forms of it an idea, accepts it for this reason, and thereby takes itself for measure, for rule, for highest authority.

After having thus proclaimed the supremacy of philosophy, we hasten to add that it is essentially tolerant. In fact, philosophy is the understanding and the explanation of all things. Of what, then, aside from error and crime, can it be the enemy? Philosophy does not combat industry, but comprehends it and refers it to principles which govern those that industry and political economy avow. Philosophy does not combat jurisprudence, but makes it the spirit of the laws. Philosophy does not cut from art its divine wings, but follows it in its flight, measures its reach and its aim. Sister of religion, it draws, from an intimate connection with her, powerful inspirations, it makes use of her sacred images, her great teachings, but at the same time it converts the truths offered to it by religion into its own substance, and into its own form: it destroys not faith; it elucidates it and promotes its growth, and raises it gently from the twilight of the symbol to the full light of pure thought.

All the wants which we have passed in review are equally specific, equally certain, equally necessary; and, reunited, they form a whole which is in some sort the entire soul of humanity. But the strength of each one of these wants is the tendency of each to realize itself separately; and they do it. Ordinarily, too ordinarily, philosophy, religion, art, the State, industry, are at variance. Far from that, true philosophy is not exclusive: it ought, on the contrary, to comprehend and draw all together. I hope that from this chair will never fall words that are hostile to whatever may be beautiful and good. It is time that philosophy, instead of forming a division in the human race, should rise above all divisions. This shall be the spirit of my teaching. This is the new character that French philosophy ought to receive at the hands of the civilization of the nineteenth century.

Young men, you who propose to frequent these lectures, love all that is good, all that is beautiful, all that is honest: here is the basis of all philosophy. Philosophy, in adding itself to them will give them its form: it will destroy nothing. Follow with interest the general movement of the physical sciences and of industry. Give to yourselves, in them, the instructive spectacle of liberty and of human intelligence, marching day by day to the conquest and dominion of the sensible world. Study the laws of our great country: imbibe in this study, with the love of these glorious laws, that of the princes who have given them to us, and who maintain them. Imbibe at the source of art and letters, the enthusiasm of all that is beautiful. Nourished in the bosom of Christianity, prepared by its noble teachings for philosophy, having arrived thus at the summit of your studies, you will find in true philosophy, with the understanding and the explanation of all things, a supreme and unalterable peace. To exclude nothing, to accept every thing, to comprehend every thing, once more, is the characteristic of our times: let this also be the character of the French youth. I will try not to be an unfaithful master to them.

The history of philosophy is necessarily relative, in a given epoch, to the state of speculative philosophy in that same epoch. This is an incontestable point; and it is still incontestable that, in every epoch, the state of speculative philosophy is relative to the general state of society. Let us apply this principle to the question which occupies us. Its first consequence is, that a new history of philosophy must result from the partial labors now everywhere in progress, and that this history of philosophy will have the same character as the speculative philosophy called to rule in the nineteenth century, and whose character appears to be eclecticism. It then remains to show that this philosophy, which already manifests itself by more than one unequivocal sign, has its necessary foundation in the present state of society in Europe.

After the great political and religious movement which had filled the sixteenth and seventeenth centuries in Europe, a new and more important movement was necessary; civilization was called to a new and more decisive movement. What, in fine, was the eighteenth century? The struggle of the old society with the new society; the very idea of the eighteenth century is the necessity of a crisis. . . .

It seems, at first view, that the Charter consecrates the social order anterior to the eighteenth century, and which the eighteenth century overturned. In short, I there behold a king, a powerful monarchy, a throne firm and respected; I there behold a Chamber of Peers invested with privileges, surrounded by universal veneration; I there see a religion which, taking our children from the cradle, teaches each one, early, his duties in this world, and the end of this life. Behold in the Charter an element which springs not from the French Revolution. It is there, nevertheless, and is necessarily there, and must be better established from day to day, and gain, continually, both respect and power. But is this the only element in the Charter? No. I see by the side of the throne a Chamber of Deputies, named directly by the people, and co-operating in the making of all the laws that establish and authorize particular measures, so that nothing is done in the remotest village of France, in which the Chamber of Deputies has not a hand. Here is an element entirely new. In the past I perceive some images of it in certain assemblies and judicial bodies; but is the image more than the reality; it is, in truth, only in the wishes of the eighteenth century, and in the irregular attempts of the French Revolution. We have then here, on one hand, an element of the ancient regime, and, on the other, an element of the revolutionary democracy. How are these elements in the Charter? In fact, they are there, and their union is so intimate, that the most skillful civilian is much embarrassed to define and limit in theory the proper action of each of these two branches of sovereign power; and there is a fortunate obscurity in regard to the right of the one and the supremacy of the other. Our glorious Constitution is no mathematical fiction of the artificial equilibrium of the legislative and executive powers, vain abstractions which should be left to the infancy of the representative government; our Constitution is the real union of the king and the people, seeking together the best manner of governing, and being useful to the common country. This is not all: in the Charter, besides the privileges of the Chamber of Peers, I find that, to all Frenchmen, there is access to all places, by virtue of which the lowest soldier, as the author himself of the Charter has said, carries the baton of the Marshal of France in his cartridge-box; and the commonest Frenchman can, in all careers, arrive even at the foot of the throne. By the side of the religion of the State, I see in characters quite as manifest, liberty of worship and liberty of the press, that is, that religious instruction is not wanting to any one, and that liberty of worship permits choice in the different communions of the Church, and that, in short, thanks to the liberty of the press, no truth being smothered, one may determine, in the sincerity of thought, in favor of opinions which seem the most true. Thus I see in the Charter all contrarieties; that is what certain people deplore: there are some who admire in our Constitution only its democratic part, and who would wish to make use of that in order to weaken all the rest; there are others who groan over the introduction of the democratic elements, and turn against them the monarchical part of the Constitution. On both sides is equal error, equal preoccupation with the past, and equal ignorance of the present. On both sides there are persons whose age is highly respectable, and who, not being the offspring of this epoch, are perfectly excusable in not comprehending the nineteenth century and its mission. But thanks to God, every thing shows that time, in its irresistible march, will unite little by little all minds and all hearts in the comprehension and love of this Charter, which contains, at the same time, the throne and the country, monarchy and democracy, order and liberty, aristocracy and equality, all the elements of history, of thoughts, and of things.

From this, I conclude, that if the French Charter contains all opposed elements founded in a harmony more or less perfect, the spirit of the Charter is (permit me the expression) a true eclecticism. This spirit, in developing itself, is applied to every thing. Already it is reflected in our literature, which contains two elements which may and ought to go together, classic legitimacy and romantic innovation. Without pursuing these applications, I ask if, when all around us is mixed, complex, and mingled together, when all contrarieties exist well together, if it is possible that philosophy should escape the general spirit? I ask if philosophy can avoid being eclectic, when all around it is so, and if, consequently, the philosophical reform undertaken in 1816, and which I shall pursue with firmness in spite of all obstacles, does not necessarily proceed from the general movement of society in all Europe, and especially in France? Eclecticism is so vigorously attacked by the double philosophy of the past, still debated in our midst, for the precise reason alone, that it is a presentiment and forerunner of the future. Eclecticism is moderation in philosophic order; and moderation which can do nothing in the days of crisis, is afterwards a necessity. Eclecticism is the necessary philosophy of the age, for it is the only one that can conform to its wants and to its spirit; and every age terminates in a philosophy which represents it. This is my most firm conviction. It is not of yesterday; and I know well it is not to be communicated in a day; I know that I am now speaking in 1828, and not in 1850.

I might say to the blind partisans of the eighteenth century: Choose among any of its theories, any of its acts, and the irresistible evidence of facts, the unanswerable authority of events sufficiently numerous, sufficiently prolonged, to enable one to see the very force and nature of things, the law of history, the judgment of Providence. Every thing was not so lawful and holy in the theories and the acts of the revolution, since of many of these theories and these acts there remains only a horrible remembrance. On the other hand, to the blind adversaries of the eighteenth century and of the great event which offers itself to them under such frightful colors, I might propose this dilemma which contains the summary of this lecture: Leave there, I would say to them, the excesses which are revolting to you, and which are revolting to me as much as to you: consider in the French Revolution its principles and its results, and then, either absolve the French Revolution, or condemn the whole age which it represents; either absolve the eighteenth century, or condemn the seventeenth, for the eighteenth is only the continuation of the seventeenth; either absolve the seventeenth century, or condemn the sixteenth, which prepared it; finally, either absolve the sixteenth century, or attach yourselves to the middle age; condemn the march and the progress of modern civilization, defend absolute immobility, oppose yourselves to history, oppose yourselves to the designs of Providence.

Besides, a higher authority has solved the question; that authority which made the Charter passed a peremptory judgment upon the eighteenth century: it discriminated between the good and the evil; it condemned what was condemnable, it consecrated what was legitimate. Every charter, every constitution, is only an historical *resume;* it is the recognition of all the essential elements of an epoch: now, the Charter recognized and placed in the first rank Christianity and royalty, which now, thanks to God, are each day taking new forces, new accessions; and for this reason the Charter confounded more than one vain theory, more than one criminal enterprise. But, at the same time, the Charter vindicated the principles and general results of the French Revolution and the eighteenth century. It not only vindicated the eighteenth century, but in vindicating that, it vindicated the two centuries which preceded and prepared it. The religious revolution of the sixteenth century was recognized and aggrandized in the Charter by the article which guaranteed liberty of worship; the political revolution of the seventeenth century was expressed in it by the introduction of a representative branch in the government of the king, and the participation of the country in the affairs of the country. The forms and even the language of the representative government of England of 1688 passed into the French Charter of 1814. You see how the sixteenth and seventeenth centuries were recognized: as to the eighteenth, the equality which had been engendered in it by the diffusion of the general principle of liberty was consecrated by the article which recognized all the French as

accessible to all employments, and which establishes the true
equality, the only possible and legitimate equality, equality before
the law; in fine, the general principle of liberty was consecrated by
the liberty of the press. What, in fact, is the liberty of the press, if
not the unlimited liberty of reasoning, the right of examination in
its entire range, that is, the principle of liberty in its highest
generality, that is, again, the entire eighteenth century? Thus the
Charter itself adopted the religious revolution of the sixteenth
century, the political revolution of the seventeenth, and the great
revolution of the eighteenth. . . .

[1826] Whether spontaneous or voluntary, all personal acts have
this characteristic in common, that they can be referred immediately to a cause which has its point of departure altogether in
itself, that is to say, that they are free; such is the proper notion of
liberty. Liberty cannot be confined to the will, for in that case,
spontaneity would not be free; and, on the other hand, liberty
cannot consist merely in spontaneity, for then the will in its turn
would not be free. If therefore the two phenomena are equally free,
they can be so only on the condition, that we discard from the
notion of liberty every thing which belongs exclusively either to
the one or the other of the two phenomena, and that we allow to it
only what is common to both. Now, what circumstance is common
to both, except that they have their point of departure in
themselves, and that they can be referred immediately to a cause,
which is their proper cause, and which acts only by its own
energy? Liberty being the common characteristic of spontaneity
and of will, comprises both these phenomena itself; it ought to
possess, and it consequently does possess, something more general
than either, and which constitutes their identity. This is the only
theory of liberty that agrees with the different facts which are
announced as free by the consciousness of the human race, and
which in their diversites have occasioned theories in contradiction
with each other, because they have been constructed exclusively
for a specific order of phenomena. Thus, for example, the theory
which concentrates liberty in the will must needs admit no other
than reflective liberty, preceded by a predetermination, accompanied with a process of deliberation, and marked with characteristics which greatly reduce the number of free acts, which take
away liberty from every thing which is not reflective, from the

enthusiasm of the poet and artist in the moment of creation, from the ignorance which reflects but little and scarcely acts otherwise than spontaneously, that is to say, from three quarters of the human race. Because the expression free-will implies the idea of choice, of comparison, and of reflection, these conditions have been imposed on liberty, of which free-will is only one form; free-will is free-volition, that is to say, volition; but will is so far from being adequate to the extent of liberty, that even language adds to it the epithet free, thus referring it to something still more general than itself. We may assert the same of spontaneity. Disengaged from the accompaniment more or less tardy of reflection, of comparison, and of deliberation, spontaneity manifests liberty in a purer form, but it is only one form of liberty, and not liberty entire; the fundamental idea of liberty is that of a power whichs, under whatever form it act, acts only by an energy peculiar to itself.

[1833] All extreme parties, therefore, are leagued against Eclecticism, under the honourable flag of the support of discord. Heaven knows what war they have waged, and with what arms! I have had the benefit of holding against me, for many years, the Sensual school and' the Theological school united. In 1830, both schools descended into the arena of politics. The Sensual school naturally produced the party of demagogues; and the Theological school quite as naturally took sides with Absolutism, except as from time to time it assumed the mask of the demagogues so as to sooner gain its ends, just as in philosophy it undertook to restore theocracy by means of scepticism. The system, on the contrary, which combated every exclusive principle in science must needs have rejected also every exclusive principle in the State, and defended Representative Government. In 1818, I gave a theory of Representative Government and of the Charter, in which I still persist. Convictions which are founded not on temporary circumstances, but on a profound study of humanity and of history, are not swept away the the wind of the first tempest. Three days have not changed the nature of things and the state of French society. Yes, as the human soul in its natural development contains many elements of which true philosophy is the harmonious expression, so every civilized society possesses many elements altogether distinct, which true government ought to recognise and represent; and the exclusive triumph of tone of these elements in a simple government, under whatever name, could be nothing but a tyranny. A mixed government is the only one appropriate to a great nation like France. The Revolution of July is merely the English Revolution of 1688, but in France,—that is to say, with far less aristocracy and a little more democracy and monarchy. The proportion of these elements may vary with circumstances; but these three elements are necessary. Let us leave republicanism to the youthful societies of America, and absolute monarchy to aged Asia. Placed between the old world and the new, at an equal distance from decrepitude and infancy, our Europe, in its vigorous maturity, contains all the elements of social life, brought to its complete development: it is therefore doomed as it were to Representative Government. This admirable form of government is a happy necessity of our times; and without the folly of proselytism, will make the tour of Europe. For France, the question I fear not to say, is that of existing in this manner, or of ceasing to exist at all. With Representative Government, I see public liberty, union, and power at home, and consequently the certain prospect of greatness and glory abroad. Let Representative Government be destroyed, and I perceive nothing but barren convulsions. civil war with foreign war. a powerless imitation of a grand epoch for ever gone by, and as a complete novelty, perhaps the dismemberment of France, and the fate of Poland and Italy. I turn my eyes from a result like this, and desire nothing that can lead to it. My political faith is therefore in entire accordance with my philosophical faith; and both the one and the other are above the outrages of party.

9   *Jean-Baptiste Say*

Jean-Baptiste Say (1767-1832) was the foremost exponent of French liberal ideas in the field of economics in the early nineteenth century. These ideas, as he himself makes clear, owe far more to Adam Smith than to his French predecessors, the Physiocrats. Say's discussion, in fact, resembles Cousin's in its historical emphasis, just as it resembles Constant's in its preoccupation with the relation between theory and practice. These may be said to be two of the characteristic marks of French as distinct from English liberalism.

Say's work, first published in 1803, was several times revised by him. The following extracts are taken from an American translation which is the only one that includes the important Introduction and incorporates the changes made in the fifth and last French edition of 1826.

About the middle of the eighteenth century, certain principles in relation to the origin of wealth, advanced by Doctor *Quesnay* made a great number of proselytes. The enthusiastic admiration manifested by these persons for the founder of their doctrines, the scrupulous exactness with which they have uniformly since followed the same dogmas, and the energy and zeal they displayed in maintaining them, have caused them to be considered as a sect, which has received the name of *economists* Instead of first observing the nature of things, or the manner in which they take place, of classifying these observations and deducing from them general propositions, they commenced by laying down certain abstract general propositions, which they styled axioms, from supposing them to certain inherent evidence of their own truth. They then endeavoured to accommodate the particular facts to them, and to infer from them their laws; thus involving themselves in the

SOURCE. *Jean-Baptiste Say, A Treatise on Political Economy; or the Production, Distribution and Consumption of Wealth,* translated by C. R. Prinsep with a translation of the Introduction and additional notes by Clement C. Biddle, Philadelphia: 1867, pp. xxxiii-xxxv, xxxvii-xxxviii, 71, 74, 86-89, 132-134, 137, 139, 175-6.

defence of maxims evidently at variance with common sense and universal experience. . . . Their opponents had not themselves formed any more correct views of the subjects in controversy. With considerable learning and talents on both sides, they were either wrong or right by chance. . . .

The economists, by promulgating some important truths, directing a more general attention to objects of public utility, and by exciting discussions, which, although at that time of no advantage, subsequently led to more accurate investigations, have unquestionably done much good. In representing agricultural industry as productive of wealth, they were not deceived; and, perhaps, the necessity they were in of unfolding the nature of production, caused the further examination of this important phenomenon, which conducted their successors to its entire development. On the other hand, the labours of the economists have been attended with serious evils; the many useful maxims they decried, their sectarian spirit, the dogmatical and abstract language of the greater part of their writings, and the tone of inspiration pervading them, gave currency to the opinion, that all who were engaged in such studies were but idle dreamers, whose theories, at best only gratifying literary curiosity, were wholly inapplicable in practice.

No one, however, has ever denied that the writings of the economists have uniformly been favourable to the strictest morality, and to the liberty which every human being ought to possess, of disposing of his person, fortune, and talents, according to the bent of his inclination; without which, indeed, individual happiness and national prosperity are but empty and unmeaning sounds. These opinions alone entitle their authors to universal gratitude and esteem. . . . This doubtless is the reason why, since the year 1760, almost all the French writers of any celebrity on subjects connected with political economy, without absolutely being enrolled under the banners of the economists, have, nevertheless, been influenced by their opinions. . . .

But none of these inquiries could lead to any important result. How, indeed, was it possible to become acquainted with the causes of national prosperity, when no clear or distinct notions had been formed respecting the nature of wealth itself?. . . In the year 1776, *Adam Smith*. . .published his *Inquiry into the Nature and Causes of the Wealth of Nations*. In this work, its author demonstrated that wealth was the exchangeable value of things; that its extent was proportional to the number of things in our possession having value; and that inasmuch as value could be given or added to matter, that wealth could be created and engrafted on things previously destitute of value, and there be preserved, accumulated, or destroyed.

In inquiring into the origin of value, Dr. Smith found it to be derived from the labour of man, which he ought to have denominated *industry,* from its being a more comprehensive and significant term than *labour.* From this fruitful demonstration he deduced numerous and important conclusions respecting the causes which, from checking the development of the productive powers of labour, are prejudicial to the growth of wealth; and as they are rigorous deductions from an indisputable principle, they have only been assailed by individuals, either too careless to have thoroughly understood the principle, or of such perverted understandings as to be wholly incapable of seizing the connexion or relation between any two ideas. Whenever the Inquiry into the Wealth of Nations is perused with the attention it so well merits, it will be perceived that until the epoch of its publication, the science of political economy did not exist.

. . .Mere unassisted industry is insufficient to invest things with value. The human agent of industry must, besides, be provided with pre-existing products; without which his agency, however skillful and intelligent, would never be put in motion. These pre-existing requisites are,

1. The tools and implements of the several arts. . . .

2. The products necessary for the subsistence of the industrious agent. . . .

3. The raw materials, which are to be converted into finished products by the means of his industry. . . .

The value of all these items constitutes what is denominated *productive capital.* . . .

Independently of the aid that industry receives from capital, that is to say, from products of her own previous creation, towards the creation of still further products, she avails herself of the agency and powers of a variety of agents not of her own creation, but offered spontaneously by nature. . . . This *process I call the productive agency of natural agents.* . . .

The labour performed by natural agents, and that executed by pre-existent products, to which we have given the name of capital, are closely analogous, and are perpetually confounded one with the other; for the tools and machines which form a principal item of capital, are commonly but expedients more or less ingenious, for turning natural powers to account. . . . Their obvious effect is to make less labour requisite for the raising the same quantity of produce, or, what comes exactly to the same thing, to obtain a larger produce from the same quantity of human labour.—And this is the grand object and the acme of industry.

Whenever a new machine, or a new and more expeditious process is substituted in the place of human labour previously in activity, part of the industrious human agents, whose service is thus ingeniously dispensed with, must needs be thrown out of employ. Whence many objections have been raised against the use of machinery. . . . Inasmuch as machinery produces that evil, it is clearly objectionable. But there are circumstances that commonly accompany its introduction, and wonderfully reduce the mischiefs, while at the same time they give full play to the benefits of the innovation. For,

1. New machines are slowly constructed, and still more slowly brought into use; so as to give time for those who are interested, to take their measures, and for the public administration to provide a remedy.

2. Machines cannot be constructed without considerable labour, which gives occupation to the hands they throw out of employ. For instance, the supply of a city with water by conduits gives increased occupation to carpenters, masons, smiths, paviours, &c. in the construction of the works, the laying down the main and branch pipes, &c. &c.

3. The condition of consumers at large, and consequently, amongst them, of the class of labourers affected by the innovation, is improved by the reduced value of the product that class was occupied upon.

Besides it would be vain to attempt to avoid the transient evil, consequential upon the invention of a new machine, by prohibiting its employment. If beneficial, it is or will be introduced somewhere or other; its products will be cheaper than those of labour conducted on the old principle; and sooner or later that cheapness will run away with the consumption and demand. . . .

So much for the immediate effect of the introduction of machinery. The ultimate effect is wholly in its favour.

Indeed if by its means man makes a conquest of nature, and compels the powers of nature and the properties of natural agents to work for his use and advantage, the gain is too obvious to need illustration. There must always be an increase of product, or a diminution in the cost of production. If the sale-price of a product do not fall, the acquisition redounds to the profit of the producer; and that without any loss to the consumer. If it do fall, the consumer is benefited to the whole amount of the fall, without any loss to the producer.

The multiplication of a product commonly reduces its price, that reduction extends its consumption; and so its production, though become more rapid, nevertheless gives employment to more hands than before. It is beyond question, that the manufacture of cotton now occupies more hands in England, France, and Germany, than it did before the introduction of the machinery that has abridged and perfected this branch of manufacture in so remarkable a degree. . . .

But however great may be the advantages, which the adventurers in industry, and even the operative classes, may ultimately derive from the employment of improved machinery, the great gain accrues to the consumers, which is always the most important class, because it is the most numerous; because it comprehends every description of producers whatever; and because the welfare of this class, wherein all others are comprised, constitutes the general wellbeing of a nation. . . .

To enable us to form clear and correct practical notions in regard to markets for the products of industry, we must carefully analyse the best established and most certain facts, and apply to them the inferences we have already deduced from a similar way of proceeding. . . .

A man who applies his labour to the investing of objects with value by the creation of utility of some sort, can not expect such a value to be appreciated and paid for, unless where other men have the means of purchasing it. Now, of what do these means consist? Of other values of other products, likewise the fruits of industry, capital, and land. Which leads us to a conclusion that may at first sight appear paradoxical, namely, that it is production which opens a demand for products. . . . Sales cannot be said to be dull because money is scarce, but because other products are so. There is always money enough to conduct the circulation and mutual interchange of other values, when those values really exist. . . . Money performs but a momentary function in this double exchange. . . .

It is quite impossible that the purchase of one product can be affected, otherwise than by the value of another.

From this important truth may be deduced the following important conclusions:—

1. That, in every community the more numerous are the producers, and the more various their productions, the more prompt, numerous, and extensive are the markets for those productions; and, by a natural consequence, the more profitable are they to the producers; for price rises with the demand. But this advantage is to be derived from real production alone, and not from a forced circulation of products; for a value once created is not augmented in its passage from one hand to another, nor by being seized and expended by the government, instead of by an individual. . . .

2. That each individual is interested in the general prosperity of all, and that the success of one branch of industry promotes that of all the others. . . .

3. From this fruitful principle, we may draw this further conclusion, that it is no injury to the internal or national industry and production to buy and import commodities from abroad; for nothing can be bought from strangers, except with native products, which find a vent in this external traffic. Should it be objected, that this foreign produce may have been bought with specie, I answer, specie is not always a native product, but must have been bought itself with the products of native industry; so that, whether the foreign articles be paid for in specie or in home products, the vent for national industry is the same in both cases.

4. The same principle leads to the conclusion, that the encouragement of mere consumption is no benefit to commerce; for the difficulty lies in supplying the means, not in stimulating the desire of consumption; and we have seen that production alone, furnishes

those means. Thus, it is the aim of good government to stimulate production, of bad government to encourage consumption.

The interference of the public authority, with regard to the details of agricultural production, has generally been of a beneficial kind. The impossibility of intermeddling in the minute and various details of agriculture, the vast number of agents it occupies, often widely separated in locality and pursuits, from the largest farming concerns to the little garden of the cottager, the small value of the produce in comparison with its volume, are so many obstacles that nature has placed in the way of authoritative restraint and interference. All governments, that have pretended to the least regard for the public welfare, have consequently confined themselves to the granting of premiums and encouragements, and to the diffusion of knowledge which has often contributed largely to the progress of this art. . . . A national administration that guards with vigilance the facility of communication and the quiet prosecution of the labours of husbandry, or punishes acts of culpable negligence, as the destroying of caterpillars and other noxious insects, does a service analogous to the preservation of civil order and of property, without which production must cease altogether. . . .

But there is no branch of industry that has suffered so much from the officious interference of authority in its details, as that of manufacture.

Much of that interference has been directed towards limiting the number of producers, either by confining them to one trade exclusively, or by exacting specific terms, on which they shall carry on their business. This system gave rise to the establishment of chartered companies and incorporated trades. The effect is always the same, whatever be the means employed. An exclusive privilege, a species of monopoly, is created, which the consumer pays for, and of which the privileged persons derive all the benefits.

10 *J. C. L. Sismondi*

J. C. L. Sismondi (1773-1842), though a Swiss, was like Rousseau, Mallet du Pan, and many others of his countrymen intensely interested and influential in France. Sismondi's influence was mainly in the field of economics, where in a pioneering work published in 1819 he attacked many of the methods, aims, and conclusions of the school of Say and laid the foundations, if not for socialism, at least, for a social approach to economics.

Sismondi arrived at this position, however, only after a long period as a disciple of Adam Smith. The book from which extracts follow dates from this period and is his first major work, completed in 1800. It is not primarily concerned with economics but with political principles, and largely for political reasons Sismondi had no success in his attempts to publish it. It was in fact never printed before the recent edition from which the following extracts are translated and therefore played no appreciable part in the development of liberalism. It is nevertheless of interest, on the one hand as an independent argument for the liberal position in the heated political debate of the period, and on the other hand precisely because in the field of economics Sismondi later felt himself obliged to abandon liberal principles while adhering to them, as his letters and later historical writings attest, in the realm of politics. In this respect his career may be compared with that of John Stuart Mill a generation later. Sismondi's version of liberalism is more democratic than that put forward by Constant, for example, and their attitudes to Rousseau differ significantly.

Since the object of my researches on free governments is to make better known the nature of liberty and the means of strengthening it, it seems proper to begin by showing exactly what liberty is. . . . Let us see whether, by going back to the beginning of societies and following the development of the rights and relations of men, we can produce a definition of liberty from its history.

SOURCE. J. C. L. Sismondi, *Recherches sur les constitutions des peuples libres.* Geneva, Droz: 1965, pp. 83-86, 96-100, 111-2, 119, 129, 134-6, 139.

In the state of nature, either before the birth of nations or after their dissolution, men enjoyed the full range of rights and prerogatives that are entailed by their absolute equality. Without laws and without earthly superiors, they recognize no other authority than that of their own interest and their reason. Nothing is forbidden to them, and their rights have no other limits than their faculties and their power.

Hunters and shepherds may remain in the state of nature for a long time. . . . But the farmer is tied to the soil and bound by his possessions. To that extent he is exposed to injury by other. . . . For such a man the freedom of the state of nature would be the worst kind of enslavement. It was therefore necessary to place limits on the freedom of action of individuals and to require a recognition of duties in exchange for the preservation of rights. Several agreements or contracts were made among neighbors or friends who wished to form a people. It is from these agreements that liberty in its various forms was born.

Society had to provide for the defense of all its members and for the preservation of its own existence. For that purpose it was necessary for men as a group to have some authority over individuals, for society to acquire some rights at the expense of its members. The first agreement among those involved defined both. But it was legitimate only so long as it did not exceed its purpose, and provided that, having made society strong enough to provide constant protection for its members, it reserved to the latter all the other rights and powers that they enjoyed in the state of nature. For *civil liberty.* . .is nothing other than the *retention in the hands of individuals of all the rights and powers that they were not necessarily obliged to give away when they formed themselves into a society.* . . .

Society could not achieve its goal and the welfare of its members without creating a government. The *social contract* had brought the people into existence, the *constitutional contract* brought the government into existence, and *democratic liberty* expressed the relation established by the *constitutional contract* between the rights of the government and those of the people.

A people must give its government all the rights and powers it needs to maintain itself and to attain the goals for which it was instituted, but the rest of the rights and powers that the individuals ceded to society had to belong to the people, and a nation could not fully enjoy its democratic liberty unless the government acquired no prerogatives beyond those necessary for its existence, all other national powers being exercised by the people themselves. We may therefore define democratic liberty as the *retention in the hands of the people of all authority that it has not necessarily been obliged to give up in order to form a government*. . . . *Civil liberty* is that of the citizens who are members of a society, *democratic liberty* is that of the citizens as members of a sovereign People. The first is the inalienable right of all men, the second is the privilege of members of a free nation. . . .

Political liberty, finally, is the principle of preserving the other two; it exists only where the nation has made sure of the security of. . .*the social contract and the constitution, and therefore of the enjoyment of the portions of civil and democratic liberty that flow from them.*

Civil liberty is violated when the people itself, or the majority of its assemblies, or its representatives or the trustees of the powers of society, encroach on the independence of individuals and arrogate to themselves prerogatives not granted to society itself.

Democratic liberty is violated when the majority of the people's assembly, or any part of the nation no matter what its size, or its magistrates, or nobles, princes, or tyrants who have come to hold the powers of government, arrogate to themselves the exercise of rights which belong to the people alone.

Political liberty, which is designed to prevent any kind of tyranny, from that of the People's Assembly to that of the despot, will therefore provide the individual with the means of resisting society in defense of the rights of man, and will provide the citizen with the means of resisting the government in defense of the rights of the people.

Political liberty is closely linked with the constitution of each State. The constitution must provide an agency for every part of the nation; it must define the people and the means by which it exercises the powers reserved to it; it must determine the prerogatives of the government and the limits which it may not exceed; and finally (and here lies the triumph of political liberty) it must establish a balance of powers such that the various members of the State reciprocally obstruct each other by their ambition, and that all are induced to work for the preservation of the social contract and the constitution.

I will therefore call *political liberty the equilibrium established by the legislator in a State, by means of which each of its parts necessarily tends to maintain the two great contracts which assure civil and democratic liberty to all. . . .*

This equilibrium. . . .cannot be established, nor can all the parts of the State and even the government by motivated to preserve the social contract, unless the people itself is invested with constitutional importance and plays a considerable part in the national balance. . . . Political liberty considered from the point of view not of its end but of its means consists, therefore, in the *Sovereignty belongs to the entire nation and not to any of its parts; its divisions being provided and combined by the constitution in such a way that none of them may be deprived of its share of sovereignty nor oppressed by the others.* . . .

Just as we have seen that civil liberty is that of individuals, and democratic liberty that of citizens, we may say that political liberty is that of the nation, for it is linked with the general constitution of the State far more than with the rights of each of the men comprised in that State. . . . Political liberty must be regarded as a dam built against the aspirations of governments of any kind. This dam is costly and can be built only at the citizens' expense, yet it must be built (though with economy) because it is useful.

A good constitution can assure to the people: (1) liberty, (2) virtue, (3) order; a good government can allow them to enjoy an administration which is (4) prudent, (5) thrifty, and (6) just. These, I think, are all the advantages that a nation can expect from the wisdom of its legislator; let us look at them in more detail.

1. Liberty. I place liberty highest among the benefits of society. . . . Civil liberty includes *personal security* against foreigners as well as against other members of the society, security of the society itself, the right *to own property and security in its tenure,* and finally *freedom of choice,* or the right to act as one wishes limited only by the need to allow the same freedom to others and not to interfere with the activity of the government. . . .

2. Virtue. . . . Political virtue. . .is found in history always attached to democratic liberty, whether because the government would fear and seek to stifle energy of this magnitude in a people which was not free, or because the great goals which are always before the eyes of a people that has a share in government are such

as to excite the higher feelings and noble enthusiasm which nourish political virtue.

3. Order. Almost all the subtlest pleasures depend on order. . . . Unfortunately, although order is not incompatible with liberty it seems to fit more easily into a more vigorous and less legitimate form of government. . . . But it is wiser to say that political liberty is always necessary to reconcile order with popular power. Political liberty, that equilibrium of powers which maintains the constitution and which preserves the State from dangerous convulsions, is essentially devoted to the maintenance of order. . . . In countries where political liberty is well established social order is always respected even in the midst of the most violent agitations, which admittedly it cannot entirely prevent.

4. Prudence. Prudence in government is not a consequence of a free constitution. . . .

5. Economy. . . . If a poor people can be both happy and free, a people impoverished by its financiers can never be. We know well that it is the freest governments which can, other things being equal, raise the highest taxes. . . .

6. Justice. The happiness of private individuals requires in a well regulated society courts capable of maintaining peace and the reign of justice. Every truly free constitution will ensure the impartiality of judges; but liberty can offer no remedy for their ignorance of the law or for their stupidity. . . .

Conclusion. . . . We may conclude that a people wishing to ensure its happiness must retain civil liberty if it wishes to taste the charms of security, property, and independence; that it must retain a share in government, or democratic liberty, if it wishes to attain virtue and to prepare itself for great actions; that it must, even at the price of some of its prerogatives, assure itself of political liberty it if wishes to enjoy the advantages of social order and tranquillity; that it must admit a certain element of aristocracy into its government if it wishes that government to be prudent and wise; and, finally, that it must neither sacrifice its liberty to finances and justice nor its finances and justice to liberty, since without a free, wise, just, and thrifty administration it is difficult to be happy.

I have thought it proper to take as the basis of my work the truths demonstrated by J. J. Rousseau in his *Social Contract* and to use them as points of departure as recognized axioms; however, I have not adopted all his principles. . . . The most important difference between his system and mine concerns the nature of the social contract. According *to him it is the turning over of every member with all his rights to the community.* I on the contrary, maintain that each member cedes only a part of his rights, in fact the smallest possible part; consequently I regard as tyrannical any usurpation by the community of all the rights of its members and especially of their personal rights. . . .

Nevertheless, I make bold to claim that even where I have appeared to move farthest away from his [Rousseau's] principles I have remained faithful to his spirit. We differ more over words than over substance. . . .

. . .The existence of various classes of citizens is a necessary consequence of the social state. . . . Once the enormous difference among men produced by nature and education is recognized, as to character and as to talents, the inequality of citizens cannot be denied. . . . Inequality of wealth and of birth likewise conflict with any attempt to establish equality of rights and powers among citizens as the basis of all free government. . . .

The differences between the poor and the rich classes. . .by no means inhibit the establishment of a free constitution which, on the contrary, by respecting and consulting them equally and balancing them off against each other, finds in them an additional support for liberty. . . . The progress of commerce and civilization have served the cause of liberty by sapping the foundations of the power that the rich had usurped in the earliest periods of society. . . .

Certain system-makers have stressed the dangers that the inequality of wealth has posed to liberty at certain periods of society and have proposed to abolish it entirely by dividing the entire wealth of the state among all citizens in equal portions and getting the very idea of property out of people's heads. . . . If the legislator contents himself with redistributing property among all citizens he will not succeed in his aim, for the multiplication of some families, the extinction of some others, industry, work, luck will within a few years, even within a few days, disturb the order he has established. . . . If the legislator wishes in addition to deprive his citizens of all right to hold property and of any possibility of acquiring it he will condemn men to indolence by destroying their most powerful motive for activity. . . .

All distinctions within a nation, whether natural or artificial, may be beneficial so long as the legislator has not emphasized or invented them save in order to allow every part of the nation as much as possible a share in sovereignty; and the distinctions are bad whenever a division established by law is in fact a discrimination against a part of the nation, for the latter, having been deprived of its legitimate share in government, will soon also be deprived of its civil liberty, to which all men have an inalienable right.

11 Felicite Robert de Lamennais

Felicite Robert de Lamennais (1782-1854) was the founder of the "liberal Catholic' movement in France. In contrast to the mainstream of liberal thought, which was not only secular but often actively anti-clerical, liberal Catholicism emphasized the spiritual freedom that men could enjoy only if their Church was free—free from interference and supervision by the state. In terms of the long history of the relations between Church and State Lamennais therefore defended what may be called the conservative, "ultramontane" position, that the papacy should not brook interference from secular rulers, against the more modern idea of national churches known in France as Gallicanism. Nevertheless, Lamennais' campaign on behalf of freedom of speech and of the press coincided with one of the central aims of secular liberals who, however, on the whole preferred a state monopoly of education to letting the Church have a share in it. Unpopular with the government, unable to form an alliance with the secular liberals, Lamennais was eventually disavowed by the pope as well who found the brilliant polemicist too volatile and embarrassing. Though dying excommunicate,

SOURCES. F. de La Mennais, *Reflexions sur l'etat de l'eglise en France pendant le dix-huitieme siecle et sur la situation actuelle suivies de melanges religieux et philosophiques,* 3rd ed., Paris and Lyon: 1821, pp. 401-2; *Des progres de la revolution et de la guerre contre l'eglise,* 2nd ed., Paris: 1829, pp. 29, 31, 36-37, 40-42, 44-46, 92-93, 97, 112-3.

Lamennais lived to see many of his ideas gain increasing acceptance. Lamennais was altogether one of the most complicated men of the century, just as "liberal Catholicism" itself suffered from a certain ineradicable element of paradox. The following extracts are taken from works published during the Restoration, before Lamennais came into open conflict with the papacy.

Beliefs and morality are in the sphere of religion; the rest is in the sphere of the individual. The rights of the government are confined to advising, guiding, offering to all without restriction the means of instruction, supervising Church establishments and even suppressing them if they are dangerous to the State or to accepted values or if they lend themselves to propagating doctrines disastrous to society. Any other rights it arrogates to itself are a usurpation of paternalistic authority.

Education is one of the principal needs of peoples, and for that reason it must be as accessible as food. Any attempt to nourish a nation administratively will result in its starving to death, whatever the finest theories may say. Let the government prevent people selling poison instead of food, let it supervise the markets with a good police force, let it even, if possible, establish stockpiles when the yield of harvests is abundant; all this is its business and even its duty. But if it goes farther, if it attempts on its own initiative to supply a whole people with bread, it will prove not its solicitude but rather its greed or its ineptitude.

Let us now consider the consequences of a restrictive regime applied to education. It places in the hands of the government, or of a few minor officials, doctrines, habits, the entire foundations of the social order. A few men, in certain circumstances a single man, will be able to impart to a whole generation his prejudices, his errors, his opinions, his passions. We have had a striking enough example of this under Bonaparte; and it is no slur on his schools to say that they were dominated with military fervor by an appalling spirit of impiety and profound immorality. I admit that all this no longer exists; but so long as education remains a monopoly of the state it could happen all over again tomorrow if tomorrow the director of public education or the head of the State were a man of the same kind; children and adolescents would once again be subjected to his opinions and whims. Unless, therefore, society itself is to be regarded as a plaything of the moment, it is worse than lack of foresight, worse than folly to make the whole social order depend on the will of one man or of a few men.

Ever since governments cut themselves off from Christianity by cutting themselves off from the Church, political society has been exposed to the activity of two doctrines in perpetual conflict in which neither of them can win a complete victory because both are in different respects equally false, equally opposed to the essential laws of the social order. The first is alleged to be the shield of the people against the tyranny of kings; the other the protection of kings against the rebellion of the people. The first [is] known by the name of liberalism . . .; the second, which is called the royalist doctrine, would be better labelled the Gallican doctrine. . . .

Let us speak first of liberalism, and begin by defining the precise sense in which we are using this word.

In periods of revolution there always appears a group of perverse individuals who take pleasure in evil for its own sake; they can breathe easily on ruins, and when they have power in their hands crime pours forth from their minds like lava from a crater. Others, occupied only with what concerns them personally, . . . foment disorder hoping to find in it opportunities favorable to their interests. Sold to whoever wants to pay them, they will today go to a club to demand the head of kings while tomorrow, kneeling before the vilest tyrant, they will be found admiring his whims and giving their blessing to his crimes. . . .

Two things constitute liberty: the legitimacy of power, and the conformity of its action to eternal justice; from this it follows that liberty is the first, the most fundamental and essential law of society. When, therefore, liberalism asks for liberty it asks for order, it asks for what nobody has the right to refuse men, for what God himself commands them to want and to love. But this same liberty that liberalism wishes for is denied by its own doctrines which inevitably lead the people into servitude.

We have said that liberty consists first of all in the legitimacy of power; nothing is more obvious. Well, the only legitimate power, as liberalism agrees, is that of God; and since it fundamentally denies the transmission of the divine power it thereby denies the possibility of a legitimate power existing among men: from which it follows that once there is a society there is servitude. . . .

Whereas liberalism is led by its doctrines to endorse either servitude or the destruction of society, Christianity, by raising man to the real source of power, establishes both society and liberty at one and the same time on an unshakable foundation.

However, the existence of liberty depends not only on the legitimacy of power but also on inviolable rules for its activity; it must govern by justice and be governed by justice. For this reason all ages and all peoples have acknowledged the existence of a *Heavenly law*, a *Divine law*, the basis of all other laws. . . . Always the same, it applies to the whole human race, which it binds together. Without it there can be no duties, no justice, no order. . . . This immutable doctrine, which neither time nor opinion can affect, constitutes the faith and the conscience of the human race. It is the warranty for its liberty: for if there is no first, universal, invariable law, which establishes rights and duties at the same time, a binding and consequently divine law, then justice is but an empty word, and the world falls victim irrecoverably to the whims of force.

Now, the most general principles of dogmatic liberalism is the sovereignty of the individual reason, or its absolute independence; a principle which, in excluding all outside authority, thereby excludes any common law, any divine and binding law, and destroys the very notion of justice and duty. . . .

We can see why liberalism, eminently social to the extent that it desires liberty, is nevertheless destructive in its action because of its doctrines which lead it astray. It rejects the bane of mankind, power without law or rules, and it demands a safeguard against arbitrary rule by undermining the habit of unquestioning obedience; so far, so good. But, cut off from the spiritual order, it is compelled to seek this much-desired safeguard where it is not and cannot be found, in the material forms of government. The fault that irritates and disturbs liberalism is inherent in the nature of the only power it is willing to recognize. It overthrows a government today for a reason which will compel it tomorrow to overthrow the one it has put in its place; and so on without end or respite.

Struck with these consequences, as disastrous as they are dangerous, of the principles of liberalism, another group of men throw themselves blindly to the opposite extreme which is no less fatal although, at the core of the errors under which it labors, there lies a just and true feeling. What, in fact, do the royalists want? A stable order, which cannot exist without obedience to power. They are therefore right to reject principles incompatible with all obedience, with all power of any kind. But to these false principles they oppose equally false ones which, moreover, violently shock the human conscience. As a result the two sides are really arguing only about fifteen modes of destruction, and it is no more possible to construct a durable society on royalist Gallican principles than on so-called liberal ones.

What are the liberals asking for? Honest implementation of the Charter that the Prince has sworn to uphold. There is nothing to object to in that.

What else do they ask for? Complementary laws in harmony with this charter which have also been promised by the Prince and on whose necessity all are agreed. There is nothing to object to in that either.

But the Charter amounts to a republic; complementary laws in harmony with the Charter can only be essentially republican laws which develop the democratic principle of institutions and cause it to penetrate by a thousand different channels into every branch of public administration. This has led to a stubborn resistance on the part of those in power, who can rely for support against legal democracy only on administrative despotism.

12   *Alphonse de Lamartine*

Alphonse de Lamartine (1790-1869), one of the greatest of French Romantic poets, was yet another man of letters who in the period of social ferment after 1815 felt the call of public affairs on his time and energy. Tempting as it is, especially in view of his exalted language, to label him a "romantic liberal," it is probably more helpful to call him an independent liberal. Although a member of the Chamber of Deputies from 1834 and generally counted on the liberal side, Lamartine never became a party man. It was his relative lack of involvement with the July Monarchy that allowed him to become a member of the Provisional Government after the Revolution in 1848, for reasons that he himself describes in the second of the following extracts. These reasons represent a considerable change of tactics, although not of general outlook, since the time of writing the long political letter of 1831 from which the first extract is translated. The nature and degree of this change tell us as much about the history of the July Monarchy and the Revolution of 1848 as about Lamartine.

When a man wishes to take into his field of vision a wider horizon he climbs up to a height proportionate to what he wants to discover; from there, he looks down and sees. This is what the philosopher must do. Let us therefore raise ourselves up to the intellectual heights from which the eye contemplates the past, dominates the present, and can detect the future. Let us shed, by dint of thought, our limitations of age, country, and period, our prejudices, our patriotic and partisan habits. . .; ley us refine ourselves down to pure intelligence, and let us look! This summit from which man can contemplate the past and future course of mankind is history; the light that must illuminate this double horizon before his eyes is morality, the divine light that comes

SOURCES. Lamartine, "Sur la politique rationnelle," in his *Oeuvres completes,* Vol. 37, Paris: 1863, pp. 358, 360-3, 365-6, 379-380; A. de Lamartine, *History of the French Revolution of 1848,* translated by Francis A. Durivage and William S. Chase, 2 vols. in 1, Boston: 1849, I, 41-45,

from God himself and that can neither mislead nor fail. In that position and by that light, with an honest heart and a clear eye, the philosopher will solve the most complex and obscure social problem that may be presented to him; he will solve it with metaphysical precision save for a margin of a few accidents and a few centuries in social change that Providence keeps for its own secret; sublime prophet of reason, he will write the history of the future!. . .

Where are we going?—The reply is contained in the present state of affairs: we are going toward one of the most sublime phases of mankind, toward a progressive and complete organization of the social order on the principle of liberty of action and equality of rights; we can foresee, for our children's children, a series of free, religious, moral, and rational centuries, an unparallelled age of truth, reason, and virtue. Or else—fatal alternative!—we will cast France and Europe into one of those chasms that often separate two epochs like an abyss separating two continents; and we shall die leaving our children a social order laid waste, new principles that are doubtful, contested, bloodstained, power impossible to wield, liberty impossible to maintain, religion persecuted or reviled, reactionary legislation, a general European war fruitless and endless, the law of the scaffold, the civilization of camps, the morality of the battlefield, the liberty of satraps, the equality of the brigand; and in the midst of all this, an idea stifled in blood, mutilated by the saber. . . . This is the choice facing us as I write to you.

What then shall we do?. . . . God, who has given man moral freedom, whom he has created to choose and to act, has at the same time given him the light to make his choice. Politics, which the ancients treated as a mystery and our contemporaries as an art, is neither one nor the other: it is neither cleverness, nor force, nor deception; in the rational epoch of the world. . .politics is morality, reason, and virtue!. . .

Your social theory will be simple and infallible: in taking God as both your point of departure and your goal, the greatest good of mankind in general as your aim, morality as your torch, conscience for your judge, and liberty for your route, you will run no risk of losing your way; you will have freed politics from the systems, the illusions, the deceptions in which passion or ignorance have encased it; you will have put it back where it belongs, in the conscience . . . .

The task of the present great age, a long, laborious, and controversial task, is to apply human reason, or the divine Word, or the truth of the gospels, to the political organization of modern societies, as the truth of the gospels was from the beginning applied to civil legislation and to social customs. . . . Politics has hitherto not been governed by God's law. The politics of Christian peoples is still pagan; man or mankind is still treated like the slaves of antiquity, born to serve, to pay, to fight, and to die!. . . Man in society must henceforth be for the philosopher and the legislator what man in isolation is for the true Christian: a son of God, having the same claims, the same rights, the same duties, the same destiny in the eyes of the terrestrial father, the State, as in the eyes of the heavenly Father, God. This is the order of things. . .that contemporaries have called democracy, by incorrect analogy with what the ancient peoples called by that name and which was in fact nothing but the tyranny of the multitude. The term democracy, soiled and bloodstained among us recently in the disorders of the French Revolution, is still repugnant to men's minds. . . . We should prefer to call this form of government the rational form or the right of all men. The rational form or the right of all men must be liberty, where everyone is the judge and guardian of his own right; therefore the modern era must be the era of liberty; its mission is to organize the rights and freedom of action of all men, in other words liberty, in a living and enduring manner. . . .

Circumstances are propitious for rigorous applications of this political philosophy to events occurring before us. The earth has trembled; an unexpected, sudden, irresistible convulsion has disturbed all interests, all passions, all affections, all systems. All is rubble, all is emptiness before us; hearts are as free as consciences; the ground is levelled as though for a grand social reconstruction prepared by the divine Architect. An ancient power, venerated by some out of conviction or nostalgia, hated by others out of impatience or prejudice, has crumbled, we may say, as a result of its own death-wish . . . . This power perished in the storm that it had itself in its blindness conjured up. We, royalists of the mind or of the heart, men of logic or of loyalty, we can only weep in silence on its scattered ruins, respect and pity the noble victims of an irrevocable mistake . . . . But, left to our own devices by a fate stronger than ourselves, we are free to act; our reason has no more bonds, our private affection no longer struggles within us against our social logic. Let us therefore, while deploring what is deplorable in this chain of centuries whose last link has broken in our hands against our wishes, know how to take advantage courageously of that liberty which catastrophe itself has given us! Let us not be guided by sentiment, which has no place in the present situation, but let us reason and act. . . .

[In his History of the Revolution of 1848 Lamartine writes about himself in the third person.]

The political principles of Lamartine were those of the eternal truth of which the gospel is a page, the equality of men in the eyes of God, realized on earth by those laws and forms of government which give to the greatest number, and presently to all citizens, the most equal share of personal participation in the government, and thence eventually in the moral and material benefits of human society.

Still Lamartine recognized the rule of reason as superior to the brutal sovereignty of numbers; for reason being in his view the reflection of God upon the human race, the sovereignty of reason was the sovereignty of God. He did not push to a chimerical point the violent and actually impossible equalization of social conditions. He could not conceive of any civilized society without three bases, which seemed given by instinct itself, that great revealer of eternal truths,—the State, Family, and Property. . . . Property, doubtless, appeared to him, like everything else, capable of being perfected by institutions which develop instead of destroying it; but the protection of wages seemed to him the freest and most perfect form of the association between capital and labor, since wages are the exacted proportion liberally estimated between the value of labor and the wants of capital—a proportion expressed in every free country by what is called common consent.

Still, as the laborer, pressed by hunger, does not possess always and immediately his perfect freedom to estimate his rights, and thus to proportion the price of his labor to the service he renders capital, Lamartine admitted, to a certain extent, the state, as the arbiter . . . between the contrary exigences of the two contracting parties.

He wished, moreover, that the state, the providence of the strong and the weak, should, in certain extreme cases, determined by the administration, furnish aid, in the shape of work, to laborers who found it utterly impossible to obtain bread for their families. He asked for a poor tax. He would not have abandonment and death the ultimatum of a civilized community to the laborer destitute of food and shelter. He would have this ultimatum—work and bread.

In fine, sensible of the advantages of property, the true civic right of modern times, he aspired to the gradual extinction of destitution, by endowing more generally with property the greatest number, and eventually all citizens. But the first condition of this successive appropriation of a portion of property to the hands of all was a respect for property in the hands of proprietors, merchants, working men already elevated by labor and inheritance to dignity and prosperity. To dispossess some to enrich others, did not seem to him progress, but an act of plunder, ruinous to all. . . .

The question of government was to Lamartine one of circumstance, rather than principle. It is evident, that if the constitutional government of Louis Philippe had honestly labored to accomplish gradually and completely the two or three moral or material measures demanded by the epoch, Lamartine would have defended the monarchy. For in his calm and rational appreciation of the happiness of nations and individuals, stability and order certainly seemed to him weighty conditions of repose. Now, repose is a good. But Lamartine knew that the *seated* powers . . . almost inflexibly refused to engage in these labors of transformation, which are almost always concussions. While himself refusing conscientiously to provoke a revolution, in his own mind he was reconciled to the perspective of an involuntary revolution, if the force of circumstances embraced one. He was resolved to brave its tempests and its perils—to direct it, on the one hand, to the accomplishment of ideas which he believed to be matured, and, on the other, confine it, as far as he could, within the limits of justice, prudence, and humanity.

The two principal ideas which Lamartine thought sufficiently pure and sufficiently matured to be worth the effort of a revolution were entirely disinterested. They concerned only the cause of God and humanity. They satisfied no personal interests or passions of his own; or, at least, they were the passions of a philosopher, and not of an ambitious man. He had nothing to gain, and much to lose by it. He only asked of this prospective revolution permission to serve it, and give his heart, his reason, and perhaps his life, to its cause. These two ideas were worthy of such a sacrifice.

One was the accession of the masses to political rights to prepare for their progressive, inoffensive, and regular advancement to justice; that is to say, to equality of standing, intelligence, relative well-being in society.

The second was the absolute emancipation of the conscience of the human race, not by the destruction but by the complete liberty, of religious creeds. The means, in his eyes, was the final separation of Church and State. . . .

Lamartine was born religious, as the air was created transparent. The sentiment of God was so inseparable from his soul, that it was impossible for him to distinguish politics from religion. All progress which did not end in a more luminous knowledge and a more active adoration of the creator, source, and end of humanity, seemed to him a groping and aimless march in nothingness.

But in calling with all his aspirations and all his acts for a progress in faith and adoration, Lamartine did not wish this progress but by the action of universal reason upon all, and of each man upon his own reason. He had a horror of persecutions, of violence, or even of the delusions of conscience. . . . He would have died for the inviolability of the sincere and conscientious worship of the last of the faithful. He desired that religions should themselves cast off the antiquity with which they were invested; he did not wish that they should be violently, or even irreverently, despoiled. His only apostle was liberty; it is the only worthy minister of God in the minds of men. He respected the priesthood, provided the priesthood was the voluntary magistracy of the soul, armed with faith, and not with law. His system of the liberty of worship by association alone was rational, pious, and opposed to revolutionary in the bad sense of that word.

These were the two secret moving principles which urged Lamartine not to make, but to accept, a revolution, or, at least, a complement of a revolution. For, he did not conceal from himself at all the difficulties, the dangers and the misfortunes, which every revolution draws after it. He loved democracy, as justice. He abhorred the principles of the demagogue, as the tyranny of the multitude. God has composed humanity, as he has composed man, of a principle of good, and of a principle of evil. There is a portion of virtue and a portion of vice and crime in the masses, as in individuals. This vice and this crime are agitated and exalted in revolutions. Everything which puts them in motion appears to multiply them, until the calm is renewed, and their nature draws them to the bottom. It is the war of the foam against the ocean. The ocean, in becoming calm, triumphs always, and swallows up the foam. But it has none the less been stained. Lamartine knew that. He trembled beforehand at the excesses of the demagogue. He was resolved to resist it, and to die, if necessary, to preserve from its delirium and its fury the pure party of the people, and the calm majesty of a revolution.

13   Francois Guizot

In juxtaposition with Lamartine, Francois Guizot (1787-1874) illustrates in many ways the width of the spectrum of liberalism in nineteenth-century France, a comparison not necessarily to Guizot's disadvantage. Ousted from his university post at the same time as Victor Cousin and joining with him in the liberal opposition to the reaction under Louis XVIII and Charles X, Guizot went on to serve the July Monarchy not only, like Cousin, as minister of education but for many years as Louis Philippe's prime minister. In this capacity he became increasingly identified with the "Party of Order" and with a policy of consolidating rather than enlarging the liberal achievement of 1830, and he was in fact leader of the government overthrown by the Revolution of 1848 that Lamartine reluctantly endorsed. In addition to being a teacher, politician, statesman, and writer of prolific and fascinating memoirs, Guizot was a man of very wide culture and knowledge and a historian of the first order whose works, particularly those revealing his deep

SOURCES. F. Guizot, Du gouvernement de la France depuis la Restauration, et du ministere actuel, 4th amended and enlarged ed., Paris: 1821, pp. 1-7, 201, 208-212; Memoirs to Illustrate the History of My Time, translated by J. W. Cole, 8 vols., London: 1858-67, I, 29-35, II, 15-24.

insight into the relevance of the British experience for France, can still be read with profit even today, though some of his historical theories are now rejected. The first of the extracts below dates from the period of Guizot's opposition immediately after his dismissal from his Chair; the second shows the light in which he viewed the Restoration and the Revolution of 1830 from the perspective of retirement. The comparative congruence between the two may be thought to show that Guizot was not, as was and still is sometimes alleged, a mere opportunist but acted throughout, for better or for worse, on consistent principles, though he may have been less ready than Lamartine to adapt to changing circumstances.

In giving France the Charter the king adopted the revolution. Adopting the revolution meant becoming the ally of his friends and the adversary of his enemies.

I use these words because they are clear and true. The revolution was a war, a real war such as has occurred in the past between different nations. For over thirteen centures France contained two races, one victor and one vanquished. For over thirteen centuries the conquered people fought to loosen the stranglehold of the victors. Our history is the history of that struggle. In our days the decisive battle was fought. It is called the revolution.

War between two peoples bearing the same name, speaking the same language, living for thirteen centuries on the same land, is a deplorable thing. Despite the causes that separate them and their constant public or private struggles the passage of time brings them closer together, mingles them, unites them with innumerable bonds, and surrounds them with a common destiny which in the end reveals only a single nation where there really still exist two distinct races, two profoundly different social situations.

Franks and Gauls, landlords and peasants, nobles and commoners, all called themselves Frenchmen long before the revolution and shared France as their common fatherland.

But time, which fertilizes everything, destroys nothing. Seeds once sown in its womb will bear fruit sooner or later. Thirteen

centuries were taken up in blending our conquering and conquered races . . . . The original division, however, negated their
course and resisted the action of the centuries. . .; and when in
1789 the deputies of all France were united in a single assembly
the two peoples were not slow to take up again their ancient
quarrel. The day of decision had finally arrived. . . .
The result of the revolution was not in doubt. The former
vanquished became the victors. They had conquered France in
their turn. In 1814 their rule was unchallenged. The charter
recognized their possession, proclaimed that this fact was law, and
provided the law with representative government as a safeguard.

The king therefore, by this single act, made himself leader of the
new conquerors. He placed himself among their ranks and at their
head, undertaking with them and on their behalf to defend the
conquests of the revolution which belonged to them.

There is no doubt that the charter contained such an undertaking, for the war was clearly about to begin again. It was easy to
predict that the conquered people would not resign themselves to
their defeat. . . . Everything that preserved for or returned to the
former possessors of privilege a gleam of hope was bound to lead
them to try to recover it. The restoration inevitably had this
effect: first, because it was a restoration, and secondly because it
reestablished liberty.

I need not insist on the first fact. Privilege had dragged the
throne to its downfall; it seemed obvious that if privilege revived,
the throne would in turn help to lift it up. . . .

But even if the events of 1814 had not led to the restoration,
even if the charter had come from another source and another
dynasty, the mere establishment of the representative system, the
very return of liberty, would have. . .recalled the erstwhile
privileged people to combat. . . . We have overcome the *ancien
regime;* we shall always overcome it; but we shall have to fight it
for a long time yet. Anyone in France who wants a constitutional
order, elections, assemblies, freedom of speech, freedom of the press,
and public liberties must not depend on. . . counter-revolution
remaining mute and inactive.

This, therefore, was the general situation in 1814. . . . Between
1814 and 1820, despite many events, oscillations, mistakes, faults,
this situation did not change. . . . In 1820 the great change took
place, the only fundamental change in six years. A ministry fell

under the blows of counter-revolution; a new ministry was formed under its influence and for its benefit. Power suddenly sought and found another group of friends. We know where they come from, and that is enough to know where they are going. . . .*

I should like to abstain from all metaphysical discussion. I believe neither in divine right nor in popular sovereignty as these are generally understood. I see in them merely usurpations of power. I believe in the sovereignty of reason, justice, and law; that is where the world will find the legitimate sovereign that it seeks and will always seek; for reason, truth, and justice are nowhere to be found in complete and infallible form. No man and no group of men possesses or can possess them without gaps or limitations. The best forms of government are those which place us most securely and allow us to advance most rapidly under the protection of those sacred values. That is the merit of representative government . . .

Revolution and counter-revolution are at present disputing over the issue of legitimacy. The former would adopt legitimacy without hesitation and even with pleasure if it could feel clearly and strongly that it was its property by conquest. The latter, knowing that it cannot live separated from legitimacy, is trying to recover and retain it and attach it to its own future. For the revolution legitimacy plays the part of a safe harbor which it would enter at full sail. For the counter-revolution it represents the last plank at which to clutch after a shipwreck.

It is perfectly obvious why in this debate revolution should be more hesitant and counter-revolution more fervent. Because of a fatal mistake, legitimacy did not separate itself from the *ancien regime* at the beginning of the battle. It allowed itself to be involved with a cause it did not share; and the revolution, on the attack and in destructive mood, struck at it with the blows that brought the *ancien regime* down. This was a great misfortune for the

*Guizot is here referring to the dismissal, after the assassination of the Duc de Berri in 1820, of the Decazes ministry and its replacement by a government headed by the Duc de Richelieu which embarked on a more reactionary policy. For further details on Guizot's relations with successive governments and the place occupied by the book from which these passages are translated see Douglas Johnson, *Guizot; Aspects of French History, 1787-1874* (London and Toronto, 1963), p. 60 and *passim.* (Editor's note.)

revolution as well as for legitimacy. This misfortune still remains with us. The presence of the Bourbons recalls memories of the *ancien regime.* . . . This is the source of the people's distrust, of their credulity, their hostility, and their obstinacy. This is the source of the uncertainty of many good citizens who desire the good of the country, entertain no hostile sentiments, and see clearly the advantages of legitimacy but cannot abandon themselves to it if they do not see legitimacy, in turn, devote itself as clearly to France. It is not enough to have received the charter from the legitimate power; proofs of the nature of legitimacy must, so to speak, be received all the time, by the attitude of the government, its acts, its language. The charter is a position that the king has taken. It is a good position, the national position. But a position needs not only to be taken once, it needs to be maintained and even reaffirmed and extended. . . . Revolution and legitimacy today have in common the fact that both are seeking to preserve themselves and to preserve the *status quo.* Neither has any need of upsetting or destroying anything; counter-revolution, by contrast, which has lost everything, wants to recover everything at the expense of revolution and to the peril of legitimacy. This alone is reason enough to tell legitimacy and revolution that their alliance is natural, necessary, and the only one profitable to them both. . . .

The present ministers are putting the throne in the position of 1791. They are leading it toward the allies who brought its ruin in ruining themselves. We demand, on the contrary, that the throne should stay on the side of the victors. Not only is this in the interest of both parties but the throne has promised it, has given itself to us. The charter is much more than a peace treaty; it is an alliance . . . . Representative government is by no means, like legitimacy, impartial and neutral by nature. It belongs to those who wanted it and won it. It is an instrument of victory and a source of security. If this instrument falls into enemy hands. . .everything is changed; what was a safeguard is turned into a threat. . . . Institutions are nothing in themselves;. . .they have a definite purpose, a practical use: they are means of attack or defense; and when power, which is the center and motive force of all institutions, has been taken over by enemies, there is only one thing that is urgent and that is to get it back.

I think, therefore, things having reached the stage where they are today, legitimacy having been put in issue between those who stand for the new France and those who stand for the *ancien regime,* that the former must have only one thought, one goal, and that is the overthrow of the system which has prevailed for the last seven months.

[From Guizot's *Memoirs.*] I have ever prized, above all other considerations, just policy, and liberty restrained by law. I despaired of both under the Empire; I hoped for them from the Restoration. . . . It is truly an absurd injustice to charge the Restoration with the presence of those foreigners which the mad ambition of Napoleon alone brought upon our soil, and which the Bourbons only could remove by a prompt and certain peace. The enemies of the Restoration, in their haste to condemn it from the very first hour, have plunged into strange contradictions. If we are to put faith in their assertions, at one time they tell us that it was imposed on France by foreign bayonets; at another, that in 1814, no one, either in France or Europe, bestowed a thought upon the subject; and again, that a few old adherences, a few sudden defections, and a few egotistical intrigues alone enabled it to prevail. Puerile blindness of party spirit! The more it is attempted to prove that no general desire, no prevailing force, from within or without, either suggested or produced the Restoration, the more its inherent strength will be brought to light, and the controlling necessity which determined the event. I have ever been surprised that free and superior minds should thus fetter themselves within the subtleties and credulities of prejudice, and not feel the necessity of looking facts in the face, and of viewing them as they really exist. In the formidable crisis of 1814, the restoration of the House of Bourbon was the only natural and solid solution that presented itself; the only measure that could be reconciled to principles not dependent on the influence of force and the caprices of human will. Some alarm might thence be excited for the new interests of French society; but with the aid of institutions mutually accepted, the two benefits of which France stood most in need, and of which for twenty-five years she had been utterly deprived, peace and liberty, might also be confidently looked for. Under the influence of this double hope, the Restoration was accomplished, not only without effort, but in despite of revolutionary remembrances, and was received throughout France with alacrity and cheerfulness. And France did wisely in this adoption, for the Restoration, in fact, came accompanied by peace and liberty. . . .

The liberty which France recovered in 1814 [was not] the triumph of any particular school in philosophy or party in politics. Turbulent propensities, obstinate theories and imaginations, at the same time ardent and idle, were unable to find in it the gratification of their irregular and unbounded appetites. It was, in truth, social liberty, the practical and legalized enjoyment of rights, equally essential to the active life of the citizens and to the moral dignity of the nation. . . .

The Senators of 1814 have been much and justly reproached for the selfishness with which, on overthrowing the Empire, they preserved for themselves, not only the integrity, but the perpetuity of the material advantages with which the Empire had endowed them;—a cynical error, and one of those which most depreciate existing authorities in the estimation of the people, for they are offensive, at the same time, to honest feelings and envious passions. The Senate committed another mistake less palpable, and more consistent with the prejudices of the country, but in my judgment more weighty, both as a political blunder, and as to the consequences involved. At the same moment when it proclaimed the return of the ancient Royal House, it blazoned forth the pretension of electing the King, disavowing the monarchical right, the supremacy of which it accepted, and thus exercising the privilege of republicanism in re-establishing the monarchy;—a glaring contradiction between principles and acts, a childish bravado against the great fact to which it was rendering homage, and a lamentable confounding of rights and ideas. It was from necessity, and not by choice, on account of his hereditary title, and not as the chosen candidate of the day, that Louis XVIII was called to the throne of France. There was neither truth, dignity, nor prudence, but in one line of conduct,—to recognize openly the royal claim in the House of Bourbon, and to demand as openly in return the national privileges which the state of the country and the spirit of the time required. Such a candid avowal and mutual respect for mutual rights, form the very essence of free government. It is by this steady union that elsewhere monarchy and liberty have developed and strengthened themselves together; and by frank co-operation, kings and nations have extinguished those internal wars which are denominated revolutions. Instead of adopting this course, the Senate, at once obstinate and timid, while wishing to place the restored monarchy under the standard of republican election, succeeded only in evoking the despotic in face of the revolutionary principle, and in raising up as a rival to the absolute right of the people, the uncontrolled authority of the King.

The Charter bore the impress of this impolitic conduct; timid and obstinate in its turn, and seeking to cover the retreat of royalty, as the Revolution had sought to protect its own, it replied to the pretensions of the revolutionary system by the pretensions of the ancient form, and presented itself as purely a royal concession, instead of proclaiming its true character, such as it really was, a treaty of peace after a protracted war, a series of new articles added by common accord to the old compact of union between the nation and the King.

In this point lay the complaint of the Liberals of the Revolution against the Charter. . . .

I do not here propose to enter upon any discussion of principles, with the apostles of absolute power; as applied to France and our own time, experience, and a very overwhelming experience, has supplied an answer. Absolute power, amongst us, can only belong to the Revolution and its representatives, for they alone can (I do not say for how long) retain the masses in their interest, by withholding from them the securities of liberty.

For the House of Bourbon and its supporters, absolute power is impossible; under them France must be free; it only accepts their government by supplying it with the eye and the hand.

The objections of the moderate party were more specious. It must be admitted that the government established by the Charter had, in its forms at least, something of a foreign aspect. Perhaps too there was reason for saying that it assumed the existence of a stronger aristocratic element in France, and of a more trained and disciplined spirit of policy, than could, in reality, be found there. Another difficulty, less palpable but substantial, awaited it; the Charter was not alone the triumph of 1789 over the old institutions, but it was the victory of one of the Liberal sections of 1789 over its rivals as well as its enemies, a victory of the partisans of the English Constitution over the framers of the Constitution of

1791, and over the republicans as well as the supporters of the ancient monarchy. . . .

But these objections had little weight in 1814. The position of affairs was urgent and imperative; it was necessary that the old monarchy should be reformed when restored. Of all the measures of improvement proposed or attempted since 1789, the Charter comprised that which was the most generally recognized and admitted by the public at large, as well as by professed politicians.

Necessity weighing equally upon all, on royalists as well as liberals, on the Duke of Orleans and on France,—the necessity of choosing between the new dynasty and anarchy,—such was, in 1830, with honest minds, uninfluenced by revolutionary passion, the determining cause of the change of government. At the critical moment, this necessity was universally felt,—by the attached friends of King Charles X., as also by the most ardent spirits of the Opposition. . . . On that day all thinking men were governed by the same conviction. Through monarchy alone France could escape from the yawning abyss, and but one monarchy was possible. . . .

In presence of this certain and urgent necessity, we were too ready to acknowledge and act on it. It is one of the chief advantages of liberal institutions, that men long accustomed to their exercise yield slowly to the yoke of emergency, and struggle much before they resign themselves to it; in such manner that reforms and revolutions are only brought about when they are really imperative and recognized beforehand by public opinion strongly tested. We were very far from that clear and determined wisdom. Our minds were full of the English Revolution of 1688, of its success, of the noble and free government it had founded, and of the glorious prosperity it had purchased for the nation. We were inspired with the ambition and hope of accomplishing a similar work, of securing the greatness with the liberty of our country, and of advancing ourselves in the pursuit of this design. We had too much confidence in our foresight and strength. We were too much occupied with the views of our own minds, and thought too little of the real state of facts around us. In 1688, there were in the constitution of society and the state of public feeling in England, means of government, and restraining points on the brink of revolution, which have no existence in France at the present day. . . . For our Revolution of 1830 we had neither the same profound causes, nor the same varied supports. We were not delivering ourselves from an intolerable tyranny. All classes were not combined in opposition to a common oppressor. We attempted a far greater enterprise with very inferior forces, much less capable either of supporting the contest with energy or of restraining it within the limits of justice and sound judgment. . . .

Not content with having a monarchy to found, we desired also to make a new constitution, and to change the Charter with the dynasty. For this, no necessity whatever existed. The Charter had passed with power and credit through the rudest trials. In spite of obstacles and hostile attempts, it had been found sufficient, during sixteen years, to defend the rights, liberties, and interests of the country. . . . We ourselves were mad enough to hurl down and rend this standard. . . .

As soon as this essentially revolutionary tendency manifested itself, the parties engaged in the great work then in progress of accomplishment, saw at once how widely they differed amongst themselves, and separated in consequence. The policy of resistance dates from the revision of the Charter. . . .

While we were deliberating, revolutionary passions and pretensions murmured round us, even to the door of our assembly-room; and beyond its walls, the new government, still unsettled and almost unknown, had neither strength nor means of action. . . . While struggling against these initiatory storms, a party began to form itself, as yet ill-combined, inexperienced, and uncertain, but seriously resolved to support constitutional monarchy, and to defend it with firmness against the spirit of revolution.

Since that epoch, and particularly since 1848, a question has been often agitated. When the Charter had been thus revised, and the Crown offered by the Chambers to the Duke of Orleans, ought we to have demanded from the people, under some form of universal suffrage, the sanction of these acts, and the acceptation of the new Charter and the new King?

If I could satisfy myself that the omission of this formality had in the slightest degree influenced, in 1848, the fall of the Government established in 1830, I should feel deep regret. . . . But the more I reflect on the subject, the more strongly I remain convinced, that the want of a vote by the nation at large occasioned no weakness to the monarchy of July during its course, and had no influence on its final reverses. The adhesion of France, in 1830, to the new Government, was perfectly free, general, and sincere. The country was more desirous of seeing it established, than jealous of an express voice in the matter; and we obeyed the true wishes, as well as the clearly understood interests of France, by putting a speedy end to the revolution, without complicated conditions or delay, and by giving a regular authority to the head of the State. But this motive, although extremely powerful, was not the only one which determined us to abstain from any appeal to popular intervention, and to wind up the drama without submitting it to the official and explicit suffrage of the public.

We believed that a monarchy was necessary to, and desired by France; and this we intended to establish. I honour a republic; it has its vices, its inherent and inevitable dangers, in common with all human institutions; but it is a noble form of government, which responds to many exigences of our nature, to many of the great interests of society, and may harmonize with the position, antecedents, and tendencies of any defined epoch or of any specific nation. I should undoubtedly have been a republican in the United States of America when they separated themselves from England. A federative republic was, for them, a natural and consistent government, the only form suited to their habits, their requirements, and their feelings. I am a monarchist in France, for the same reasons and the same interests. As a republic was to the United States in 1776, so is a monarchy, in our days, the obvious and true system for France, the most favourable to public liberty and peace, the best suited for the development of salutary and legitimate strength, and for the repression of perverse and destructive agencies.

Alexis de Tocqueville (1805-1859) is probably the most famous of all French liberals, particularly in America because much of his most acute analysis is contained in the comparisons between France and the United States in his pioneering Democracy in America. *His work on the French ancien regime is, however, equally important for an understanding of the liberal mentality and is, moreover, still a significant work of history. His memoirs* (Recollections), *like Guizot's, afford further insight and a comparison between his contemporaneous and retrospective judgments.*

Tocqueville, like Guizot and Lamartine, was an active politician and statesman as well as a man of letters. In the spectrum of liberal politics he occupied a position between those of Lamartine and Guizot and his memoirs, incidentally, offer a penetrating explanation of the failure of liberalism in power under Guizot's leadership. After many years as a deputy under the July Monarchy, despite his disillusionment with the Revolution of 1848 of which he also writes in the Recollections, *he served briefly as foreign minister under Louis Napoleon in 1849 but became finally convinced even before the latter's coup d'etat of 1851 that the Second Republic would issue in despotism.*

[From Democracy in America, *first published in 1835 and 1840. In the countries in which the doctrine of the sovereignty of the people ostensibly prevails, the censorship of the press is not only dangerous, but it is absurd.*

SOURCES. *Alexis de Tocqueville,* Democracy in America, translated by Henry Reeve, edited with an Introduction by Henry Steele Commager, New York and London: Oxford University Press, 1947, pp. 103-4, 109-115, 162-9, 308, 310, 493-507; Used by permission. *The Ancien Regime and the French Revolution,* translated by Stuart Gilbert, with an Introduction by Hugh Brogan, London: Collins, 1966, pp. 27-31, 142-3, 178-9, 183, 185-8; copyright 1955 by Doubleday & Company, Inc. Reprinted by permission of Doubleday & Company, Inc. and William Collins Sons & Co. Ltd. *Recollections,* translated by Alexander Teixeira de Mattos, edited with many additions and notes by J. P. Mayer, London: Harvill Press, 1948, pp. 2-4, 7-10, 68-72. Reprinted by permission of Columbia University Press and The Harvill Press Ltd.

When the right of every citizen to cooperate in the government of society is acknowledged, every citizen must be presumed to possess the power of discriminating between the different opinions of his contemporaries, and of appreciating the different facts from which inferences may be drawn. The sovereignty of the people and the liberty of the press may therefore be looked upon as correlative institutions; just as the censorship of the press and universal suffrage are two things which are irreconcilably opposed, and which cannot long be retained among the institutions of the same people. Not a single individual of the twelve millions who inhabit the territory of the United States has as yet dared to propose any restrictions to the liberty of the press. . . .

America is perhaps, at this moment, the country of the whole world which contains the fewest germs of revolution; but the press is not less destructive in its principles than in France, and it displays the same violence without the same reasons for indignation. In America, as in France, it constitutes a singular power, so strangely composed of mingled good and evil that it is at the same time indispensable to the existence of freedom, and nearly incompatible with the maintenance of public order. Its power is certainly much greater in France than in the United States; though nothing is more rare in the latter country than to hear of a prosecution having been instituted against it. The reason of this is perfectly simple; the Americans, having once admitted the doctrine of the sovereignty of the people, apply it with perfect consistency. . . .

In no country in the world has the principle of association been more successfully used, or more unsparingly applied to a multitude of different objects, than in America. Besides the permanent associations which are established by law under the names of townships, cities, and counties, a vast number of others are formed and maintained by the agency of private individuals.

The citizen of the United States is taught from his earliest infancy to rely upon his own exertions in order to resist the evils and the difficulties of life; he. looks upon social authority with an eye of mistrust and anxiety, and he only claims its assistance when he is quite unable to shift without it. . . . The same spirit pervades every act of social life. . . .

The more we consider the independence of the press in its principal consequences, the more are we convinced that it is the chief and, so to speak, the constitutive element of freedom in the modern world. A nation which is determined to remain free is therefore right in demanding the unrestrained exercise of this independence. But the unrestrained liberty of political association cannot be entirely assimilated to the liberty of the press. The one is at the same time less necessary and more dangerous than the other. A nation may confine it within certain limits without forfeiting any part of its self-control; and it may sometimes be obliged to do so in order to maintain its own authority. . . .

It must be acknowledged that the unrestrained liberty of political association has not hitherto produced, in the United States, those fatal consequences which might perhaps be expected from it elsewhere. The right of association was imported from England, and it has always existed in America; so that the exercise of this privilege is now amalgamated with the manners and customs of the people. At the present time the liberty of association is become a necessary guarantee against the tyranny of the majority. In the United States, as soon as a party is become preponderant, all public authority passes under its control; its private supporters occupy all the places, and have all the force of the administration at their disposal. As the most distinguished partisans of the other side of the question are unable to surmount the obstacles which exclude them from power, they require some means of establishing themselves upon their own basis, and of opposing the moral authority of the minority to the physical power which domineers over it. Thus a dangerous expedient is used to obviate a still more formidable danger.

The omnipotence of the majority appears to me to present such extreme perils to the American republics that the dangerous measure which is used to repress it seems to be more advantageous than prejudicial. . . . There are no countries in which associations are more needed, to prevent the despotism of faction or the arbitrary power of a prince, than those which are democratically constituted. In aristocratic nations the body of the nobles and the more opulent part of the community are in themselves natural associations, which act as checks upon the abuses of power. In countries in which these associations do not exist, if private individuals are unable to create an artificial and a temporary substitute for them, I can imagine no permanent protection against the most galling tyranny; and a great people may be oppressed by a small faction, or by a single individual, with impunity. . . .

It cannot be denied that the unrestrained liberty of association for political purposes is the privilege which a people is longest in learning how to exercise. If it does not throw the nation into anarchy, it perpetually augments the chances of that calamity. On one point, however, this perilous liberty offers a security against dangers of another kind; in countries where associations are free, secret societies are unknown. In America there are numerous factions, but no conspiracies.

The most natural privilege of man, next to the right of acting for himself, is that of combining his exertions with those of his fellow creatures, and of acting in common with them. I am therefore led to conclude that the right of association is almost as inalienable as the right of personal liberty. No legislator can attack it without impairing the very foundations of society. Nevertheless, if the liberty of association is a fruitful source of advantages and prosperity to some nations, it may be perverted or carried to excess by others, and the element of life may be changed into an element of destruction. . . .

In a country like the United States, in which the differences of opinions are mere differences of hue, the right of association may remain unrestrained without evil consequences. The inexperience of many of the European nations in the enjoyment of liberty leads them only to look upon the liberty of association as a right of attacking the Government. The first notion which presents itself to a party, as well as to an individual, when it has acquired a consciousness of its own strength, is that of violence: the notion of persuasion arises at a later period and is only derived from experience. The English, who are divided into parties which differ most essentially from each other, rarely abuse the right of association, because they have long been accustomed to exercise it. . . .

But perhaps the most powerful of the causes which tend to mitigate the excesses of political association in the United States is Universal Suffrage. In countries in which universal suffrage exists the majority is never doubtful, because neither party can pretend to represent that portion of the community which has not voted. The associations which are formed are aware, as well as the nation at large, that they do not represent the majority: this is, indeed, a condition inseparable from their existence: for if they did represent the preponderating power, they would change the law instead of soliciting its reform. The consequence of this is that the moral influence of the Government which they attack is very much increased, and their own power is very much enfeebled. . . .

Unlimited power is in itself a bad and dangerous thing; human beings are not competent to exercise it with discretion, and God alone can be omnipotent, because his wisdom and his justice are always equal to his power. But no power upon earth is so worthy of honor for itself, or of reverential obedience to the rights which it represents, that I would consent to admit its uncontrolled and all-predominant authority. When I see that the right and the means of absolute command are conferred on a people or upon a king, upon an aristocracy or a democracy, a monarchy or a republic, I recognize the germ of tyranny, and I journey onward to a land of more hopeful institutions.

In my opinion the main evil of the present democratic institutions of the United States does not arise, as is often asserted in Europe, from their weakness, but from their overpowering strength; and I am not so much alarmed at the excessive liberty which reigns in that country as at the very inadequate securities which exist against tyranny.

When an individual or a party is wronged in the United States, to whom can he apply for redress? If to public opinion, public opinion constitutes the majority; if to the legislature, it represents the majority, and implicitly obeys its injunctions; if to the executive power, it is appointed by the majority, and remains a passive tool in its hands; the public troops consist of the majority under arms; the jury is the majority invested with the right of hearing judicial cases; and in certain States even the judges are elected by the majority. . . .

It is in the examination of the display of public opinion in the United States that we clearly perceive how far the power of the majority surpasses all the powers with which we are acquainted in Europe. Intellectual principles exercise an influence which is so invisible, and often so inappreciable, that they baffle the toils of oppression. At the present time the most absolute monarchs in Europe are unable to prevent certain notions, which are opposed to their authority, from circulating in secret throughout their dominions, and even in their courts. Such is not the case in America; as long as the majority is still undecided, discussion is carried on; but as soon as its decision is irrevocably pronounced, a submissive silence is observed, and the friends, as well as the opponents, of the measure unite in assenting to its propriety. The reason of this is perfectly clear: no monarch is so absolute as to combine all the powers of society in his own hands, and to conquer all opposition with the energy of a majority which is invested with the right of making and of executing the laws. . . .

I know no country in which there is so little true independence of mind and freedom of discussion as in America. . . .In America, the majority raises very formidable barriers to the liberty of opinion: within these barriers on authority may write whatever he pleases, but he will repent it if he ever steps beyond them. Not that he is exposed to the terrors of an *auto-da-fe,* but he is tormented by the slights and persecutions of daily obloquy. His political career is closed forever, since he has offended the only authority which is able to promote his success. Every sort of compensation, even that of celebrity, is refused to him. Before he published his opinions he imagined that he held them in common with many others; but no sooner has he declared them openly then he is loudly censured by his overbearing opponents, while those who think like him, without having the courage to speak, abandon him in silence. He yields at length, oppressed by the daily efforts he has been making, and he subsides into silence, as if he was tormented by remorse for having spoken the truth . . . .

Monarchical institutions have thrown an odium upon despotism; let us beware lest democratic republics should restore oppression, and should render it less odious and less degrading in the eyes of the many, by making it still more onerous to the few . . . .

The tendencies to which I have just alluded are as yet very slightly perceptible in political society, but they already begin to exercise an unfavorable influence upon the national character of the Americans. I am inclined to attribute the singular paucity of distinguished political characters to the ever-increasing activity of the despotism of the majority in the United States . . . .In that immense crowd which throngs the avenues to power in the United States I found very few men who displayed any of that manly candor and that masculine independence of opinion which frequently distinguished the Americans in former times, and which constitutes the leading feature in distinguished characters, wheresoever they may be found. It seems, at first sight, as if all the minds of the Americans were formed upon one model, so accurately do they correspond in their manner of judging . . . . If ever the free institutions of America are destroyed, that event may be attributed to the unlimited authority of the majority, which may at some future time urge the minorities to desperation, and oblige them to have recourse to physical force. Anarchy will then be the result, but it will have been brought about by despotism. . . .

Although men cannot become absolutely equal unless they be entirely free, and consequently equality, pushed to its farthest extent, may be confounded with freedom, yet there is good reason for distinguishing the one from the other. The taste which men have for liberty, and that which they feel for equality, are, in fact, two different things . . . .

I think that democratic communities have a natural taste for freedom: left to themselves, they will seek it, cherish it, and view any privation of it with regret. But for equality, their passion is ardent, insatiable, incessant, invincible: they call for equality in freedom; and if they cannot obtain that, they still call for equality in slavery. They will endure poverty, servitude, barbarism—but they will not endure aristocracy. This is true at all times, and especially true in our own. All men and all powers seeking to cope with this irresistible passion will be overthrown and destroyed by it. In our age, freedom cannot be established without it, and despotism itself cannot reign without its support . . . .

I believe that it is easier to establish an absolute and despotic government among a people in which the conditions of society are equal, than among any other; and I think that if such a government were once established among such a people, it would not only oppress men but would eventually strip each of them of several of the highest qualities of humanity. Despotism, therefore, appears to me peculiarly to be dreaded in democratic ages. I should have loved freedom, I believe, at all times, but in the time in which we live I am ready to worship it. On the other hand, I am persuaded that all who shall attempt, in the ages upon which we are entering, to base freedom upon aristocratic privilege, will fail—that all who shall attempt to draw and to retain authority within a single class, will fail. At the present day no ruler is skilful or strong enough to found a despotism, by re-establishing permanent distinctions of rank among his subjects: no legislator is wise or powerful enough to preserve free institutions if he does not take equality for his first principle and his watchword. All those of our contemporaries who would establish or secure the independence and the dignity of their fellowmen must show themselves the friends of equality; and the only worthy means of showing themselves as such, is to be so: upon this depends the success of their holy enterprise. Thus the question is not how to reconstruct aristocratic society, but how to make liberty proceed out of that democratic state of society in which God has placed us.

These two truths appear to me simple, clear, and fertile in consequences; and they naturally lead me to consider what kind of free government can be established among a people in which social conditions are equal.

It results from the very constitution of democratic nations and from their necessities that the power of government among them must be more uniform, more centralized, more extensive, more searching, and more efficient than in other countries. Society at large is naturally stronger and more active, individuals more subordinate and weak; the former does more, the latter less; and this is inevitably the case. It is not, therefore, to be expected that the range of private independence will ever be as extensive in democratic as in aristocratic countries—nor is this to be desired; for, among aristocratic nations, the mass is often sacrificed to the individual, and the prosperity of the greater number to the greatness of the few. It is both necessary and desirable that the government of a democratic people should be active and powerful: and our object should not be to render it weak or indolent, but solely to prevent it from abusing its aptitude and its strength
. . . .

I think that men living in aristocracies may, strictly speaking, do without the liberty of the press: but such is not the case with those who live in democratic countries. To protect their personal independence I trust not to great political assemblies, to parliamentary privilege, or to the assertion of popular sovereignty. All these things may, to a certain extent, be reconciled with personal servitude—but that servitude cannot be complete if the press is free: the press is the chiefest democratic instrument of freedom.

Something analogous may be said of the judicial power

. . . .The strength of the courts of law has ever been the greatest security which can be offered to personal independence; but this is more especially the case in democratic ages: private rights and interests are in constant danger, if the judicial power does not grow more extensive and more strong to keep pace with the growing equality of conditions.

Equality awakens in men several propensities extremely dangerous to freedom, to which the attention of the legislator ought constantly to be directed. I shall only remind the reader of the most important among them. Men living in democratic ages do not readily comprehend the utility of forms: they feel an instinctive contempt for them . . . .Yet this objection which the man of democracies make to forms is the very thing which renders forms so useful to freedom; for their chief merit is to serve as a barrier between the strong and the weak, the ruler and the people, to retard the one, and give the other time to look about him. Forms become more necessary in proportion as the government becomes more active and more powerful, while private persons are becoming more indolent and more feeble. Thus democratic nations naturally stand more in need of forms than other nations, and they naturally respect them less . . . .Another tendency, which is extremely natural to democratic nations and extremely dangerous, is that which leads them to despise and undervalue the rights of private persons. . . .

I shall conclude by one general idea . . . .In modern society everything threatens to become so much alike that the peculiar characteristics of each individual will soon be entirely lost in the general aspect of the world. Our forefathers were ever prone to make an improper use of the notion that private rights ought to be respected; and we are naturally prone, on the other hand, to exaggerate the idea that the interest of a private individual ought always to bend to the interest of the many. The political world is metamorphosed: new remedies must henceforth be sought for new disorders. To lay down extensive, but distinct and settled limits, to the action of the government; to confer certain rights on private persons, and to secure to them the undisputed enjoyment of those rights; to enable individual man to maintain whatever independence, strength, and original power he still possesses; to raise him by the side of society at large, and uphold him in that position—these appear to me the main objects of legislators in the ages upon which we are now entering . . . .

I trace among our contemporaries two contrary notions which are equally injurious. One set of men can perceive nothing in the principle of equality but the anarchical tendencies which it engenders: they dread their own free agency—they fear themselves. Other thinkers, less numerous but more enlightened, take a different view: beside that track which starts from the principle of equality to terminate in anarchy, they have at last discovered the road which seems to lead men to inevitable servitude. They shape their souls beforehand to this necessary condition; and, despairing of remaining free, they already do obeisance in their hearts to the master who is soon to appear. The former abandon freedom, because they think it dangerous; the latter, because they hold it to be impossible. If I had entertained the latter conviction, I should not have written this book, but I should have confined myself to deploring in secret the destiny of mankind. I have sought to point out the dangers to which the principle of equality exposes the independence of man, because I firmly believe that these dangers are the most formidable, as well as the least foreseen, of all those which futurity holds in store: but I do not think that they are insurmountable. The men who live in the democratic ages upon which we are entering have naturally a taste for independence: they are naturally impatient of regulation, and they are wearied by the permanence even of the condition they themselves prefer. They are fond of power; but they are prone to despise and hate those who wield it, and they easily elude its grasp by their own mobility and insignificance. These propensities will always manifest themselves, because they originate in the groundwork of society, which will undergo no change: for a long time they will prevent the establishment of any despotism, and they will furnish fresh weapons to each succeeding generation which shall struggle in favor of the liberty of mankind. Let us then look forward to the future with that salutary fear which makes men keep watch and ward for freedom, not with that faint and idle terror which depresses and enervates the heart.

[From *The Ancien Regime and the French Revolution*, first published in 1856.] In tracing the course of the Revolution I shall draw

attention to the events, mistakes, misjudgments which led
. . .Frenchmen to abandon their original ideal and, turning their
backs on freedom, to acquiesce in an equality of servitude under
the master of all Europe. I shall show how a government, both
stronger and far more autocratic than the one which the Revolution had overthrown, centralised once more the entire administration, made itself all-powerful, suppressed our dearly bought
liberties, and replaced them by a mere pretence of freedom; how
the so-called "sovereignty of the people" came to be based on the
votes of an electorate that was neither given adequate information
nor an opportunity of getting together and deciding on one policy
rather than another; and how the much vaunted "free vote" in
matters of taxation came to signify no more than the meaningless
assent of assemblies tamed to servility and silence. Thus the nation
was deprived both of the means of self-government and of the chief
guarantee of its rights, that is to say the freedom of speech,
thought, and literature which ranked among the most valuable
and noblest achievements of the Revolution . . . .

There may be some to accuse me of making overmuch of
liberty—that watchword of the past. Nowadays, so I am told, no
one in France sets any store on it. All I would say (for what it is
worth) in my defence is that my devotion to freedom is of very
long standing . . . .

Though there can be no certainty about the future, three facts
are plain to see in the light of past experience. First, that all our
contemporaries are driven on by a force that we may hope to
regulate or curb, but cannot overcome, and it is a force impelling
them, sometimes gently, sometimes at headlong speed, to the
destruction of aristocracy. Secondly, that those peoples who are so
constituted as to have the utmost difficulty in getting rid of
despotic government for any considerable period are the ones in
which aristocracy has ceased to exist and can no longer exist.
Thirdly, that nowhere is despotism calculated to produce such evil
effects as in social groups of this order; since, more than any other
kind of regime, it fosters the growth of all the vices to which they
are congenitally prone . . . .

Freedom and freedom alone can extirpate these vices, which,
indeed, are innate in communities of this order; it alone can call a
halt to their pernicious influence. For only freedom can deliver the
members of a community from that isolation which is the lot of the

individual left to his own devices and, compelling them to get in touch with each other, promote an active sense of fellowship. In a community of free citizens every man is daily reminded of the need of meeting his fellow men, of hearing what they have to say, or exchanging ideas, and coming to an agreement as to the conduct of their common interests. Freedom alone is capable of lifting men's minds above mere mammon worship and the petty personal worries which crop up in the course of everyday life, and of making them aware at every moment that they belong each and all to a vaster entity, above and around them—their native land. It alone replaces at certain critical moments their natural love of material welfare by a loftier, more virile ideal; offers other objectives than that of getting rich; and sheds a light enabling all to see and appraise men's vices and their virtues as they truly are.

True, democratic societies which are not free may well be prosperous, cultured, pleasing to the eye, and even magnificent, such is the sense of power implicit in their massive uniformity; in them may flourish many private virtues, good fathers, honest merchants, exemplary landowners, and good Christians, too . . . .But, I make bold to say, never shall we find under such conditions a great citizen, still less a great nation; indeed, I would go so far as to maintain that where equality and tyranny coexist, a steady deterioration of the mental and moral standards of a nation is inevitable.

Such were my views and thus I wrote twenty years ago, and nothing that has taken place in the world since then has led me to change my mind. And, having proclaimed my love of freedom at a time when it was made much of, I can hardly be blamed for championing it today, when it is out of fashion.

Any notion that the old order was one of servility and subservience is very wide of the mark. There was far more freedom in that period than there is today, but it was a curiously ill-adjusted, intermittent freedom, always restricted by class distinctions and tied up with immunities and privileges. Though it enabled Frenchmen on occasion to defy the law and to resist coercion, it never went so far as to ensure even the most natural and essential rightsl to all alike. Yet partial and perverse though it was, this freedom served France well. At the very time when the forces of centralisation were deliberately crushing out all individuality and trying to impose a drab uniformity, a sort of dingy monochrome, this spirit of independence kept alive in many individuals their sense of personality and encouraged them to retain their colour and relief. More than this, it fostered a healthy self-respect and often an overmastering desire to make a name for themselves. This is why we find in eighteenth-century France so many outstanding personalities, those men of genius, proud and greatly daring, who made the Revolution what it was: at once the admiration and the terror of succeeding generations. It would be absurd to suppose that such virile virtues could have sprung from a soil on which all liberty had been extinguished.

But though this peculiar, ill-assimilated, and, as it were, unwholesome liberty prepared the French for the great task of overthrowing despotism, it made them by the same token less qualified than perhaps any other nation to replace it by stable government and a healthy freedom under the sovereignty of law
. . . .

It is a remarkable fact that of all the ideas and aspirations which led up to the Revolution the concept and desire of political liberty, in the full sense of the term, were the last to emerge, as they were also the first to pass away . . . .

Towards the middle of the eighteenth century a group of writers known as the "Physiocrats" or "Economists", who made the problems of public administration their special study, came on the scene. Though the Economists figure less prominently than our philosophers in histories of the period and perhaps did less than they towards bringing about the Revolution, I am inclined to think it is from their writings that we learn most of its true character. In dealing with the problems of government the philosophers confined themselves for the most part to general ideas and purely abstract theories; the Economists, while never losing sight of theory, paid more heed to practical politics . . . .

The form of tyranny sometimes described as "democratic despotism" (it would have been unthinkable in the Middle Ages) was championed by the Economists well before the Revolution. They were for abolishing all hierarchies, all class distinction, all differences of rank, and the nation was to be composed of individuals almost exactly alike and unconditionally equal. In this undiscriminated mass was to reside, theoretically, the sovereign power; yet it was to be carefully deprived of any means of controlling or even supervising the activities of its own government. For above it was a single authority, its mandatory, which was entitled to do anything and everything in its name without consulting it. This authority could not be controlled by public opinion since public opinion had no means of making itself heard; the State was a law unto itself and nothing short of a revolution could break its tyranny . . . .

In the mid-eighteenth century the French people, if consulted, would have shown no more enthusiasm than the Economists for liberty; it was something they had quite lost touch with, indeed the very idea of freedom meant nothing to them. What they wanted was not so much a recongiiton of the "rights of man" as reforms in the existing system, and had there then been on the throne a monarch of the calibre and temperament of Frederick the Great, he would certainly have initiated many of the sweeping changes made by the Revolution in social conditions and the government of the country, and thus not only have preserved but greatly added to his power . . . .

Twenty years later things were very different. By now the idea of freedom had found its way into the minds of Frenchmen and was appealing to them more and more. . . .The French now wanted something more than ameliorations in the existing system; they wished to get the administration into their own hands. And it was clear that the gigantic revolution that now was getting under way would be carried out not merely with the consent but with the active help of the populace at large.

I am convinced that from this moment the far-reaching political upheaval which was to sweep away without distinction both what was worst and what was best in the old system became inevitable. A nation so unused to acting for itself was bound to begin by wholesale destruction when it launched into a programme of wholesale reform. An absolute monarch would have been a far less dangerous innovator. Personally, indeed, when I reflect on the way the French Revolution, in destroying so many institutions, ideas, and customs inimical to freedom, abolished so many others which were indispensable to freedom, I cannot help feeling that had this revolution, instead of being carried out by the masses on behalf of the sovereignty of the people, been the work of an enlightened autocrat, it might well have left us better fitted to develop in due course into a free nation . . . .

By the time their ancient love of freedom reawakened in the hearts of the French, they had already been inoculated with a set of ideas as regards the way the country should be governed that were not merely hard to reconcile with free institutions but practically ruled them out. They had come to regard the ideal social system as one whose aristocracy consisted exclusively of government officials and in which an all-powerful bureaucracy not only took charge of affairs of State but controlled men's private lives. Desirous though they were of being free, they were unwilling to go back on the ideology described above and merely tried to adjust it to that of freedom.

This they proposed to do by combining a strong central administration with a paramount legislative assembly: the bureaucratic system with government by the electorate. The nation as a whole had sovereign rights, while the individual citizen was kept in strictest tutelage; the former was expected to display the sagacity and virtues of a free race, the latter to behave like an obedient servant.

It was this desire of grafting political liberty on to institutions and an ideology that were unsuited, indeed adverse to it, but to which the French had gradually become addicted—it was this desire of combining freedom with the servile state that led during the last sixty years to so many abortive essays of a free regime followed by disastrous revolutions. The result has been that, wearied of these vain attempts and the efforts involved, many Frenchmen have lost their taste for freedom and come to think that, after all, an autocratic government under which all men are equal has something to be said for it.

[From the *Recollections,* written in 1850-51.] Our history from 1789 to 1830, viewed from a distance and as a whole, affords as it were the picture of a struggle to the death between the Ancien Regime, its traditions, memories, hopes, and men, as represented by the aristocracy, and the New France led by the Middle Class. The year 1830 closed the first period of our revolutions, or rather of our revolution: for there is but one, which has remained always the same in the face of varying fortunes, of which our fathers witnessed the beginning, and of which we, in all probability, shall not live to see the end. In 1830 the triumph of the middle class had been definite and so thorough that all political power, every prerogative, and the whole government was confined and, as it were, heaped up within the narrow limits of this one class . . . .Not only did it thus rule society, but it may be said to have formed it. It entrenched itself in every vacant place, prodigiously augmented the number of places and accustomed itself to live almost as much upon the Treasury as upon its own industry.

No sooner had the Revolution of 1830 become an accomplished fact, than there ensued a great lull in political passion, a sort of general subsidence, accompanied by a rapid increase in public wealth. The particular spirit of the middle class became the general spirit of the government . . . .an active, industrious spirit, often dishonourable, generally orderly, occasionally reckless through vanity or egoism, but timid by temperament, moderate in all things except in its love of ease and comfort, and last but not least mediocre . . . .Master of everything in a manner that no aristocracy has ever been or may ever hope to be, the middle class, when called upon to assume the government, took it up as an industrial enterprise; it entrenched itself behind its power, and before long, in their egoism, each of its members thought much more of his private business than of public affairs; of his personal enjoyment than of the greatness of the nation.

Posterity, which sees none but the more dazzling crimes, and which loses sight, in general, of mere vices, will never, perhaps, know to what extent the government of that day, towards its close, assumed the ways of an individual enterprise, which conducts all its transactions with a view to the profits accruing to the sharehol-ders . . . .

In this political world thus constituted and conducted, what was most wanting, particularly towards the end, was political life itself. It could neither come into being nor be maintained within the legal circle which the Constitution had traced for it: the old aristocracy was vanquished, the people excluded. As all business was discussed among members of one class, in the interest and in the spirit of that class, there was no battlefield for contending parties to meet upon. This singular homogeneity of position, of interests, and consequently of views, reigning in what M. Guizot had once called the legal country, deprived the parlimentary debates of all originality, of all reality, and therefore of all genuine passion . . . .

On the other hand, the preponderating influences which King

Louis-Philippe had acquired in public affairs, which never permitted the politicians to stray very far from that Prince's ideas, lest they should at the same time be removed from power, reduced the different colours of parties to the merest shades, and debates to the splitting of straws. I doubt whether any parliament (not excepting the Constituent Assembly . . .of 1789) ever contained more varied and brilliant talents than did ours during the closing years of the Monarchy of July. Nevertheless, I am able to declare that these great orators were bored to death of listening to one another, and, what was worse the whole country was bored of listening to them . . . .The country . . .conceived for [the governing class] a silent contempt, which was generally taken for confiding and contented submission.

The country was at that time divided into two unequal parts, or rather zones; in the upper, which alone was intended to contain the whole of the nation's political life, there reigned nothing but languor, impotence, stagnation, and boredom; in the lower, on the contrary, political life began to make itself manifest by means of feverish and irregular signs, of which the attentive observer was easily able to seize the meaning.

I was one of these observers; and although I was far from imagining that the catastrophe was so near at hand and fated to be so terrible, I felt a distrust springing up and insensibily growing in my mind, and the idea taking root more and more that we were making strides towards a fresh revolution. This denoted a great change in my thoughts; since the general appeasement and flatness that followed the Revolution of July had led me to believe for a long time that I was destined to spend my life amid an enervated and peaceful society. Indeed, anyone who had only examined the inside of the governmental fabric would have had the same conviction. Everything there seemed combined to produce with the machinery of liberty a preponderance of Royal power which verged upon despotism . . . .King Louis-Philippe was persuaded that, so long as he did not himself lay hand upon that fine instrument, and allowed it to work according to rule, he was safe from all peril. His only occupation was to keep it in order, and to make it work according to his own views, forgetful of society, upon which this ingenious piece of mechanism rested; he resembled the man who refused to believe that his house was on fire, because he had the key to it in his pocket. I could neither have the same interests nor the same cares, and this permitted me to see through the mechanism of institutions and the agglomeration of petty every-day facts, and to observe the state of morals and opinions in the country. There I clearly saw the appearance of several of the portents that usually denote the approach of revolutions, and I began to believe that in 1830 I had taken for the end of the play what was nothing more than the end of an act.

[At this point in his *Recollections* Tocqueville inserts several of his speeches and writings of 1847 and early 1848 to support his claim to have predicted the revolution.]

The Revolution of February [1848], in common with all other great events of this class, sprang from general causes, impregnated, if I am permitted the expression, by accidents . . . .

The industrial revolution which, during the past thirty years, had turned Paris into the principal manufacturing city of France and attracted within its walls an entire new population of workmen . . . tended more and more to inflame this multitude. Add to this the democratic disease of envy, which was silently permeating it; the economical and political theories which were beginning to make their way and which strove to prove that human misery was the work of laws and not of Providence, and that poverty could be suppressed by changing the conditions of society; the contempt into which the governing class, and especially the men who led it, had fallen, a contempt so general and so profound that it paralyzed the resistance even of those who were most interested in maintaining the power that was being overthrown; the centralization which reduced the whole revolutionary movement to the overmastering of Paris and the seizing of the machinery of government; and lastly, the mobility of all this, institutions, ideas, men and customs, in a fluctuating state of society which had, in less than sixty years, undergone the shock of seven great revolutions, without numbering a multitude of smaller, secondary upheavals. These were the general causes without which the Revolution of February would have been impossible. The principal accidents which led to it were the passions of the dynastic Opposition, which brought about a riot in proposing a reform; the suppression of this riot, first over-violent and then abandoned; the sudden disappearance of the old Ministry, unexpectedly snapping the threads of power, which the new ministers, in their confusion, were unable either to seize upon or to reunite;

the mistakes and disorder of mind of these ministers, so powerless to re-establish that which they had been strong enough to overthrow; the vacillation of the generals; the absence of the only princes who possessed either personal energy or popularity; and above all, the senile imbecility of King Louis-Phillippe, his weakness, which no one could have foreseen, and which still remains almost incredible, after the event has proved it.

I have sometimes asked myself what could have produced this sudden and unprecedented depression in the King's mind. Louis-Philippe had spent his life in the midst of revolutions, and certainly lacked neither experience, courage, nor readiness of mind. . . .In my opinion, his weakness was due to his excessive surprise; he was overwhelmed with consternation before he had grasped the meaning of things. The Revolution of February was unforeseen by all, but by him more than any other; he had been prepared for it by no warning from the outside, for since many years his mind had withdrawn into that sort of haughty solitude into which in the end the intellect almost always settles down of princes who have long lived happily, and who, mistaking luck for genius, refuse to listen to anything, because they think that there is nothing left for them to learn from anybody. Besides, Louis-Philippe had been deceived, as. . .his ministers were, by the misleading light cast by antecedent facts upon present times. One might draw a strange picture of all the errors which have thus been begotten, one by the other, without resembling each other-. . . .Lastly, Louis-Philippe, who had more perspicacity [than any of the kings who have been victims of revolutions], imagining that, in order to remain on the Throne, all he had to do was to observe the letter of the law while violating its spirit, and that, provided he himself kept within the bounds of the Charter, the nation would never exceed them. To warp the spirit of the Constitution without changing the letter; to set the vices of the country in opposition to each other; gently to drown revolutionary passion in the love of material enjoyment: such was the idea of his whole life. Little by little, it had become, not his leading, but his sole idea. He had wrapped himself in it, he had lived in it; and when he suddenly saw that it was a false idea, he became like a man who is awakened in the night by an earthquake, and who, feeling his house crumbling in the darkness, and the very ground seeming to yawn beneath his feet, remains distracted amid this unforeseen and universal ruin . . . .

It was the second revolution I had seen accomplish itself, before my eyes, within seventeen years! On the 30th of July, 1830, at daybreak, I had met the carriages of King Charles X on the outer boulevards of Versailles, with damaged escutcheons, proceeding at a foot pace, in Indiàn file, like a funeral, and I was unable to restrain my tears at the sight. This time my impressions were of another kind, but even keener. Both revolutions had afflicted me; but how much more bitter were the impressions caused by the last! I had until the end felt a remnant of hereditary affection for Charles X; but that King fell for having violated rights that were dear to me, and I had every hope that my country's freedom would be revived rather than extinguished by his fall. But now this freedom seemed dead; the Princes who were fleeing were nothing to me, but I felt that the cause I had at heart was lost.

I had spent the best days of my youth amid a society which seemed to increase in greatness and prosperity as it increased in liberty; I had conceived the idea of a balanced regulated liberty, held in check by religion, custom and law; . . .it had become the passion of my life. . . .

I had gained too much experience of men to be able to content myself with empty words; I knew that, if one great revolution is able to establish liberty in a country, a number of succeeding revolutions make all regular liberty impossible for very many years.

I could not yet know what would issue from this last revolution, but I was already convinced that it could give birth to nothing that would satisfy me; and I foresaw that, whatever might be the lot reserved for our posterity, our own fate was to drag on our lives miserably amid alternate reactions of licence and oppression.

PART II
Commentaries

15   *F.-A. Mignet*

Francois Auguste Marie Mignet (1796-1884) was the first professional historian to write a history of the French Revolution from a liberal (and rather optimistic) standpoint. As such it is worth noting, even though Cousin, Lamartine, Guizot, Tocqueville, and indeed almost all commentators and actors on the French scene ever since the Revolution, whatever their place in the political spectrum, have almost inevitably had to use the Revolution as a point of departure and reference.

I propose to sketch rapidly the history of the French revolution, which stands at the beginning of the period of new societies in Europe as the English revolution began the period of new governments. This revolution not only altered political power but also changed the whole internal life of the nation. The forms of medieval society were previously still in existence. The land was divided into hostile provinces, men were divided into rival classes. The nobility had lost all its powers but kept its honors; the people possessed no rights, the monarchy was unlimited, and France was

SOURCE: F. A. Mignet, *Histoire de la Revolution Francaise, depuis 1789 jusqu'en 1814,* 12th ed., Brussels and Frankfurt: 1844 (first published 1824), pp. 1-3, 9-11, 150-3.

the victim of ministerial whims, private government, and corporate privileges. The revolution replaced this abusive order with one more in conformity with justice and more appropriate to our times. It replaced arbitrary power by law, privilege by equality; it freed men from class distinctions, the land from provincial barriers, industry from the obstacles presented by corporations and guilds, agriculture from feudal servitude and oppressive tithes, property from the constraints of entail; and it brought everything together under a single state, a single law, a single nation.

On the way to achieving such great reforms the revolution had many obstacles to overcome, which were the cause of temporary excesses to be set off againt its permanent benefits. The privileged classes sought to prevent the revolution, Europe tried to suppress it, and, forced to fight for survival, the revolution could neither limit its own efforts nor enjoy victory with restraint. The domestic resistance led to the sovereignty of the multitude, and the external aggression to military domination. Nevertheless the aim was attained, despite both anarchy and despotism; the old society was destroyed during the revolution, and the new one established under the empire.

When a reform has become necessary and the moment for its achievement has arrived nothing can stop it and everything works in its favor. At such a time would be fortunate if they could come to an agreement—if those who had too much gave it up and those in want did not demand more than they needed; revolutions would take place in a friendly spirit, and the historian would have no excesses and no misfortunes to record; he would have only to show mankind wiser, freer, and happier. But history has hitherto offered no example of this sort of prudent sacrifices: those who ought to make them refuse; those tho desire them impose them; and good employs the same means as evil—violence and usurpation. There has never yet been a sovereign other than force . . . .

I propose to explain the various crises of the revolution . . .These various phases were almost inevitable, in view of the irresistible power of the events that produced them. Perhaps it would be bold to assert that things could not have turned out differently; but what is certain is that, taking account of the causes that led to it and the passions that it used and aroused, the revolution was bound to take this course and lead to this result. In sketching the prelude to the revolution I shall hope to show that it was no longer possible either to prevent it or to guide it . . .

The time for *coups d'etat* was over. Arbitrary royal power was so discredited that the king hesitated to risk using it and met with disapproval even at court. A new power had come into being, the power of public opinion which, though not recognized, was nonetheless influential and whose judgments began to be decisive. Up to this time the nation was recovering its rights little by little; it did not share power but modified it. This is the course taken by all power in the ascendant . . .The time when the Third Estate was to enter upon a share in government had at last arrived. It had made attempts earlier which were fruitless because premature. . .At last, after a century of absolute subjection, it reentered the arena, acting for the first time in its own behalf. The past cannot be revived, and it was no more possible then for the nobility to recover from its earlier defeat than it is possible at the present day for the monarchy. A different adversary confronted the court . . ., the Third Estate, whose power, wealth, stability, and intelligence were growing daily . . .

The court itself had contributed to the progress of the Third Estate and to one of its principal instruments, the Enlightenment. The most absolute of monarchs [i.e. Louis XIV] had helped along the growing mental restlessness and unintentionally created public opinion. In encouraging eulogy he laid the basis for condemnation . . .When the hymns of praise had died down analysis began, and the philosophers of the eighteenth century replaced the men of letters of the seventeenth. Everything became the object of their researches and their reflections—governments, religion, laws, abuses. They discovered rights, revealed needs, pointed out injustices. A strong and enlightened public opinion was formed directing some of its thrusts at the government which, however, did not dare to stifle it. It even converted those whom it attacked: courtiers and governors, the former as a matter of good manners and the latter as one of necessity, submitted to its decisions, and the century of reforms was prepared by the century of philosophy as the latter had been prepared by the century of the fine arts.

The constitution of 1791 was fashioned according to principles that corresponded to the ideas and situation of France. This constitution was the work of the middle class, at that time the strongest; for, as everyone knows, the dominant power always seizes control of institutions . . .Equality among citizens was pronounced right, and delegation of powers was established . . . .

According to this constitution the people were the source of all power but did not exercise any; . .their governing officials were chosen by an electorate restricted to the enlightened. The latter also manned the assembly, the courts, the administrative offices, local government, and the National Guard, and in this way controlled all the force and power in the state. They were at that time alone qualified to control them because they alone had the intelligence necessary for the conduct of government. The people were far from advanced enough yet to have a share of power; it was therefore only by accident and temporarily that they acquired it; but they were receiving an education in civic matters and practice in government in the primary assemblies, as is appropriate to the true aim of society which is not to hand over its advantages to one class as a hereditary right but rather to let them all share in them when they are capable of gaining them. This was, indeed, the principal distinguishing feature of the constitution of 1791; in proportion as someone became suitable for possessing a right he was given it. The constitution expanded its framework with the progress of civilization, which day by day attracts a larger number of men to public administration. In this way the constitution established true equality, whose real hallmark is admissibility as that of inequality is exclusion. By making power responsive to elections it turned it into a public office, whereas privilege, which transmits power by heredity, makes a private property of it.

The constitution of 1791 established a parity of powers which were related to and limited one another; it must be said, however, that the authority of the king was too much subordinated to popular power . . . . This constitution was, nevertheless, less democratic than that of the United States, which was practicable despite the extent of the territory; which proves that it is not the form of institutions but the consent they obtain or the dissent they provoke that permits or prevents their establishment. In a new country after a revolution for independence, as in America, any constitution is possible; there is only one enemy, the mother country, and as soon as this is defeated the battle ceases because its defeat entails its expulsion. This does not apply to social revolutions among peoples with a long history. Changes affect vested interests, the vested interests form parties, the parties begin to fight, and the clearer the victory the greater the resentments it provokes: this is what happened to France. The work of the Constituent Assembly perished less because of its defects than because of blows dealt by various factions. Caught between the aristocracy and the multitude it was attacked by the one and invaded by the other. The latter would not have become sovereign if the civil war and the foreign coalition had not required its intervention and help. If it was to defend the country it required to govern it; so it made its own revolution just as the middle class had done.

16   Hippolyte Taine

Hippolyte Taine (1828-1893), a literary critic and philosopher of the first rank as well as a historian, in contrast to Mignet (though much later) presents a pessimistic view of the Revolution and one hostile to the liberals, whom he depicts as misled by Enlightenment ideology.

Towards the end of 1789, moderate people, who are minding their own business, retire into privacy, and are daily less disposed to show themselves. The public square is occupied by others who, through zeal and political passion, abandon their pursuits, and by those who, finding themselves hampered in their social sphere, or repelled from ordinary circles, were merely awaiting a new opening to take a fresh start. In these utopian and revolutionary times, there is no lack of either class. . . .During the second half of the year 1790 we see them everywhere following the example of the Paris Jacobins, styling themselves friends of the Constitution, and

SOURCE: H. A. Taine, *The Revolution,* translated by John Durand, Vol. I, London: 1878, pp. 209-216.

grouping themselves together in popular associations. Each town and village gives birth to a club of patriots who regularly every evening, or several times a week, meet "for the purpose of cooperating for the safety of the commonwealth." This is a new and spontaneous organ, an excrescence and a parasite, which develops itself in the social body alongside of its legal organizations. Its growth insensibly increases, attracting to itself the substance of the others, employing them for its own ends, substituting itself for them, acting by and for itself alone, a sort of omnivorous outgrowth the encroachment of which is irresistible, not only because circumstances and the working of the Constitution nourish it, but also because its germ, deposited at a great depth, is a living portion of the Constitution itself.

For, placed at the head of the Constitution, as well as of the decrees which are attached to it, stand the Declaration of the Rights of Man.—According to this, and by the avowal of the legislators themselves, there are two parts to be distinguished in the law, the one superior, eternal, inviolable, which is the self-evident principle, and the other inferior, temporary, and open to discussion, which comprehends more or less exact or erroneous applications of this principle. No application of the law is valid if it derogates from the principles. No institution or authority is entitled to obedience if it is opposed to the rights which it aims to guarantee. These sacred rights, anterior to all society, take precedence of every social convention, and whenever we would know if a legal order is legitimate, we have merely to ascertain if it is in conformity with natural right. Let us, accordingly, in every doubtful or difficult case, refer to this philosophic gospel, to this incontestable catechism, this primordial creed proclaimed by the National Assembly.—The National Assembly itself invites us to do so. For it announces that "ignorance, neglect, or contempt of the rights of man are the sole causes of public misfortune, and of the corruption of governments." It declares that "the object of every political association is the preservation of natural and imprescriptible rights." It enunciates them, "in order that the acts of legislative power and the acts of executive power may at once be compared with the purpose of every political institution." It desires "that every member of the social body should have its declaration constantly in mind."—Thus we are told to control all acts of application by the principle, and also we are provided with the rule by which we may and should accord, measure, or even refuse our submission to, deference for, and toleration of established institutions and legal authority.

What are these superior rights, and, in case of dispute, who will decide as arbitrator? There is nothing here like the precise declarations of the American Constitution, those positive prescriptions which serve to sustain a judicial appeal, those express prohibitions which prevent beforehand certain species of laws from being passed, which prescribe limits to public powers, which mark out the province not to be invaded by the State because it is reserved to the individual.

On the contrary, in the declaration of the National Assembly, most of the articles are abstract dogmas, metaphysical definitions, more or less literary axioms, that is to say, more or less false, now vague and now contradictory, open to various interpretations and to opposite constructions, good for platform display but bad in practice, mere stage effect, a sort of pompous standard, useless and heavy, which, hoisted in' front of the Constitutional house and shaken every day by violent hands, cannot fail soon to tumble on the heads of the passers-by. Nothing is done to ward off this visible danger. . . .

Consider, indeed, these rights as they are proclaimed, along with the commentary of the haranguer who expounds them at the club before an audience of heated and daring spirits, or in the street to the rude and fanatical multitude. Every article in the Declaration is a dagger pointed at human society, and the handle has only to be pressed to make the blade enter the flesh. Among "these natural and imprescriptible rights" the legislator has placed "resistance to oppression." We are oppressed: let us resist and take up arms. According to this legislator, "society has the right to bring every public agent of the Administration to account." Let us away to the Hotel-de-Ville, and interrogate our lukewarm or suspected magistrates, and watch their sessions to see if they prosecute priests and disarm the aristocrats; let us stop their intrigues against the people; let us force these slow clerks to hasten their steps.— According to this legislator "all citizens have the right to take part in person, or through their representatives, in the formation of the law." There must thus be no more electors privileged by their payment of a three-franc tax. Down with the new aristocracy of active citizens! Let us restore to the two millions of proletaires the right of suffrage, of which the Constitution has unjustly defrauded them!—According to this legislator, "men are born and remain free, and equal in their rights." Consequently, let no one be excluded from the National Guard; let everybody, even the pauper, have some kind of weapon, a pike or gun, to defend his freedom!—In the very terms of the Declaration "there is no longer hereditary right to any public office." Hereditary royalty is therefore illegitimate; let us go to the Tuileries and overthrow the throne! In the very terms of the Declaration "the law is the expression of the universal will." Listen to these clamours in the open streets, to these petitions flowing in from the towns on all sides; behold the universal will, the living law which abolishes the written law! On the strength of this the leaders of a few clubs in Paris are to depose the King, to violate the Legislative Assembly and decimate the National Convention.—In other terms, the turbulent, factious minority is to supplant the sovereign nation, and henceforth there is nothing to hinder it from doing what it pleases just when it pleases. The operation of the Constitution has given to it the reality of power, while the preamble of the Constitution clothes it with the semblance of right.

Such is the work of the Constituent Assembly. In several of its laws, especially those which relate to private interests, in the institution of civil regulations, in the penal and rural codes, in the first attempts at, and the promise of, a uniform civil code, in the enunciation of a few simple regulations regarding taxation, procedure, and administration, it planted good seed. But in all that relates to political institution and social organization its proceedings are those of an academy of Utopians, and not those of practical legislators.—On the sick body intrusted to it, it performed amputations which were as useless as they were excessive, and applied bandages as inadequate as they were injurious. With the exception of two or three restrictions admitted inadvertently, and the maintenance of the show of royalty, also the obligation of a small electoral qualification, it carried out its principle to the end, the principle of Rousseau. It deliberately refused to consider man as he really was under its own eyes, and persisted in seeing nothing in him but the abstract being created in books. Consequently, with the blindness and obstinacy characteristic of a speculative surgeon, it destroyed, in the society submitted to its scalpel and to its theories, not only the tumours, the enlargements, and the inflamed parts of the organs, but also the organs themselves, and even the vital governing centres around which the cells arrange themselves to recompose an injured organ.

That is, the Assembly destroyed on the one hand the time-honoured, spontaneous, and lasting societies formed by geographical position, history, common occupations and interests, and on the other, those natural chiefs whose name, repute education, independence, and earnestness designated them as the best qualified to occupy high positions. In one direction it despoils and permits the ruin and proscription of the superior class, the nobles, the members of Parliament, and the upper middle class. In another it dispossesses and breaks up all historic or natural corporations, religious congregations, clerical bodies, providences, parliaments, societies of art and of all other professions and pursuits. . . . .As awkward in destruction as it is in construction, it invents for the restoration of order in a society which is turned upside down a machine which would, of itself, create disorder in a tranquil society. . . . .The masterpiece of ideal abstractions and of practical absurdities is perfected; spontaneous anarchy, by means of the Constitution, becomes legalised anarchy.

17   *Duvergier de Hauranne*

Prosper Duvergier de Hauranne (1798-1881), himself an active liberal deputy, in the introduction and conclusion of his detailed and impressive history of parliamentary government in France provides an objective assessment, spiced with personal feeling, of the nature and extent of the liberal achievement between 1814 and 1830.

The history of parliamentary government in France can be separated into two distinct periods with 1830 as the caesura. In

SOURCE: Duvergier de Hauranne, *Histoire du gouvernement parlementaire en France, 1814-1848,* (10 vols., Paris: 1857-71, I, x-xiii, X, 703-5.

1814 parliamentary government was converted from theory into practice, from a revolutionary to a legal status, and took on a regular form; then, on a day of crisis, March 20, 1815, its most outspoken enemies, the Comte d'Artois and Napoleon, the Ultra-royalists and the Bonapartists, attached themselves to it with more or less sincerity. A few months later, after a great disaster, it faltered for a moment only to recover and, in the course of a curious struggle, to acquire its most essential principles at the hands of the very men who had been hostile to it and who would soon try to destroy it. Then, between September 5, 1816 and February 13, 1820 it overcame most of the obstacles placed in its way on behalf of a number of very different passions and endowed France with a wise and liberal series of laws. At this point one of those crimes took place which, by the just dispensation of Providence, damage the cause they are designed to serve and further the cause they are designed to destroy. Although innocent of this crime committed in its name liberty suffered the penalty, and parliamentary government declined into obscurity until it revived stronger and brighter than ever in 1827 when France wakened from a long sleep and at last understood where she was being led. From that day the decisive battle was joined between the parliamentary and monarchical principles, the preponderance of representative assemblies and that of the king, and the nation, consulted as required by law, pronounced in favor of the parliamentary principle and legislative assemblies. At this point the king, instead of accepting the sovereign decision of the nation as he was required to do by the Charter, attempted to overturn this decision by force, and the force to which he appealed turned against him.

In 1830 parliamentary government, after many tribulations, many struggles, many vicissitudes, therefore won a complete victory, and the first period of its history was ended. Then the second began, that of the internal difficulties it encountered, of the convulsions that took place in its midst, of the mistakes that it was induced to commit, of the accidents that surprised and undermined it, and finally of its downfall. . . .

The government of 1830, the ministry and the opposition, did not concern themselves sufficiently with what the masses of the people felt, thought, and wanted. This was how the ground was cut from under our feet while we were politely fencing with each other, and how we ended up blindfold in a catastrophe expected by nobody, including those who brought it about and profited from it. When absolute governments perish in this way nobody can be surprised. Free governments, however, have the duty and the means to be more sensitive and perceptive about what is in the wind. But even in free government there is sometimes an inclination to be lulled into obtuseness by success and to go to sleep while sitting on power. Then it can happen that, out of fear of going too fast, one decides to stop going altogether, and such a gulf is opened up between the rulers and the ruled that they lose sight of each other. Then nothing more than an accident and a spark is needed to set off an explosion. . . .

The Charter of 1814 contained the first real and practical organization of parliamentary government; but the Charter of 1814, which people like to portray as springing fully drafted from the head of Louis XVIII was, on the contrary, the result and, in a way, the summary of ideas suggested earlier and of systems already in existence.

All France had rallied enthusiastically to the new regime [in 1830],. . .but the dissensions that were soon to divide opinion among the victors began to appear almost at once, and people began to discuss whether the new Chamber of Deputies should continue its work or give way to a different one. On one side the working population continued to agitate; the crucial question of wages was debated in clubs and in the streets; there were some instances of refusal to pay indirect taxes. It was therefore easy to foresee that, after the first days had passed, parties would form and fight again. Nevertheless, between the republican minority and the legitimist minority, the national and constitutional majority was so strong that there was every promise of a long life for the parliamentary monarchy. . . .

It remains to decide whether the revolution could have ended differently and whether, as more than one politician still believes, it would have been wise to accept [Charles X's] abdication and place the young heir of the old dynasty on the throne. This is, however, an untenable opinion, given color by our misfortunes but incapable of withstanding serious examination. Two principles were at war; one of them had to succumb, and any peace that would have been made would have been broken at the first opportunity. Anyway, such a peace would have been impossible in view of the way people were thinking. . . .

Between the republic which was impossible, and legitimate monarchy which was no longer possible, what better solution was there than this parliamentary monarchy, a true republic with a hereditary president which, if properly understood and loyally operated, provided the country with the means of governing itself and of smoothly achieving any political or social progress? No doubt it would be absurd to claim that this fornm of goverment is the only one that could realize the ideal that France had been pursuing in vain for eighty years, and that the union of order and liberty could not also be accomplished under a carefully considered republican form. But those who founded the parliamentary monarchy in 1830 had every reason to believe that in so doing they are founding the government most suitable for France and that this government would last. It did not, and history will decide to whom its fall should chiefly be attributed.

18   *Lord Acton*

Lord Acton (1834-1902), lecturing at Cambridge University at the very end of the nineteenth century, presented the classic defense of the liberal position during the French Revolution from the point of view of an English Whig, reacting sharply against criticisms such as those of Taine, whom he castigated in his inimitable style as "not a historian, but a pathologist." A Roman Catholic, Acton was especially interested in moral and religious aspects of history as well as political. The career and personality of the constitutional monarchist Count Mirabeau confronted him with a particularly fascinating problem.

SOURCE: John Emerich Edward Dalberg-Acton, First Baron Acton, *Lectures on the French Revolution,* ed. John Neville Figgis and Reginald Vere Laurence, New York: St. Martin's Press, Inc., 1959, pp. 142-4, 153, 156-8. Reprinted by permission of St. Martin's Press, Inc., and Macmillan, London and Basingstoke.

By the compulsory removal [of the government from Versailles] to Paris [October, 1789] the democracy became preponderant. They were strengthened by the support of organized anarchy outside, and by the disappearance of their chief opponents within. Mounier was the first to go. The outrage at Versailles had occurred while he presided, and he resigned his seat with indignation. . . .His example was followed by a large number of moderate men, who despaired of their country, and who, by declining further responsibility, helped to precipitate the mischief they foresaw.

The constitutional cause, already opposed by Conservatives, was now deserted by the Liberals. . . .The Left were now able to carry out in every department of the State their interpretation of the Rights of Man. They were governed mainly by two ideas. They distrusted the king as a malefactor, convicted of the unpardonable sin of absolutism, whom it was impossible to subject to too much limitation and control; and they were persuaded that the securities for individual freedom which are requisite under a personal government are superfluous in a popular community conducting its affairs by discussion and compromise and adjustment, in which the only force is public opinion. The two views tended to the same practical result—to strengthen the legislative power, which is the nation, and weaken the executive power, which is the king. To arrest this tendency was the last effort that consumed the life of Mirabeau. The danger that he dreaded was no longer the power of the king, but the weakness of the king.

The old order of things had fallen, and the customary ways and forces were abolished. The country was about to be governed by new principles, new forms, and new men. All the assistance that order derives from habit and tradition, from local connection and personal credit, was lost. Society had to pass through a dangerous and chaotic interval, during which the supreme need was a vigorous administration. That is the statesmanlike idea which held possession of Mirabeau, and guided him consistently through the very tortuous and adventurous course of his last days. He had no jealousy of the Executive. Ministers ought to be chosen in the Assembly, ought to lead the Assembly, and to be controlled by it; and then there would be no motive to fear them and to restrict their action. That was an idea not to be learnt from Montesquieu, and generally repudiated by theorists of the separation of powers.

It was familiar to Mirabeau from his experience of England, where, in 1784, he had seen the country come to the support of the king against the parliament. Thence he gathered the conception of a patriot king, of a king the true delegate and mandatory of the nation, in fact of an incipient Emperor. If his schemes had come to anything, it is likely that his democratic monarch might have become as dangerous as any arbitrary potentate could be, and that his administration would have proved as great an obstacle to parliamentary government as French administration has always been since Napoleon. But his purpose at the time was sincerely politic and legitimate, and he undertook alone the defence of constitutional principles. During the month of September Mirabeau raised the question of a parliamentary Ministry, both in the press and in the Assembly. He prepared a list of eminent men for the several offices, assigning to himself a seat in the Cabinet without a portfolio. . . .The Ministers of the day did not trust him,. . .and in their aversion for him, and for his evident self-seeking, they carried a motion forbidding deputies to take office. By this vote, of November 7, which permanently excluded Mirabeau from the councils of the king, the executive was deprived of authority. It is one of the decisive acts of the Constituent Assembly, for it ruined the constitutional monarchy.

[Mirabeau continued, however, to work for constitutional monarchy and throughout 1790 was an adviser at court.]

Mirabeau triumphed. He had opposed the assignats at first. . . .He now changed his attitude. He not only affirmed that the Church lands would be adequate security for paper, making it equivalent to gold, but he was willing that the purchase money should be paid in assignats, doing away with bullion altogether. But the cloven hoof appeared when he assured the king that the plan which he defended would fail, and would involve France in ruin. He meant that it would ruin the Assembly, and would enable the king to dissolve. The same Machiavellian purpose guided him in Church questions. He was at heart a Liberal in matters of conscience, and thought toleration too weak a term for the rights inseparable from religion. But he wished the constitutional oath to be imposed with rigour, and that the priests should be encouraged to refuse it. . . .

Mirabeau never swerved from the fundamental convictions of 1789. . . . Odious as he was, and foredoomed to fail, he was yet the supreme figure of the time. Tocqueville, who wrote the best book, or one of the two best books, on the subject, looking to the permanent result, describes the Revolution as having continued and completed the work of the monarchy by intensifying the unity of power. It is more true to say that the original and essential spirit of the movement was decentralisation—to take away from the executive government, and to give to local authorities. The executive could not govern, because it was obliged to transmit orders to agents not its own, whom it neither appointed nor dismissed nor controlled. The king was deprived of administrative power, as he had been deprived of legislative power. That distrust, reasonable in the old regime, ought to have ceased, when the Ministers appointed by the king were deputies presented by the Assembly. That was the idea by which Mirabeau would have preserved the Revolution from degenerating through excess of decentralisation into tyranny. As a Minister, he might have saved the Constitution. 'It is not to the discredit of the Assembly that the horror which his life inspired made his genius inefficient, and that their labours failed because they deemed him too bad for power.

If Mirabeau is tried by the test of public morals, the only standard of political conduct on which men may be expected to agree, the verdict cannot be doubtful. His ultimate policy was one vast intrigue, and he avowedly strove to do evil that good might come. . . .

The answer is different if we try him by a purely political test, and ask whether he desired power for the whole or freedom for the parts. Mirabeau was not only a friend of freedom, which is a term to be defined, but a friend of federalism, which both Montesquieu and Rousseau regarded as the condition of freedom. When he spoke confidentially, he said that there was no other way in which a great country like France could be free. If in this he was sincere, and I believe that he was sincere, he deserves the great place he holds in the memory of his countrymen.

19   *Benedetto Croce*

*Benedetto Croce (1866-1952), the great Italian philosopher, critic, and
historian, was a staunch anti-Fascist and a leading apostle of liberalism not
merely for Italy but on a world-wide scale. While believing in an ultimately
inevitable liberal triumph he acutely discerned the weaknesses of the liberal
movement in France and elsewhere. His historical work ranged from
philosophical inquiries into the nature of history and historiography to an
unsurpassed book on the history of Naples, where he lived most of his life and
where in 1931 he delivered the lectures from which the following extracts are
taken.*

Since. . .the liberal ideal at this time [1830] had an actual and
not merely a theoretical preponderance over the others, and if the
better and more combative forces were on its side and bent and
dominated the opposing forces not from the outside but from the
inside, what was the July Revolution? . . . The moment when the
struggle that in varying shape and with varying rhythm had lasted
for years, between liberalism and absolutism, turned into an
armed conflict, in which the two hostile parties respectively
affirmed the same character that had appeared in the preceding
events, and in that very fact, and by means of the conflict, the one
increased the energy that is possessed, and the other diminished
and lost its own, and was defeated.

With it, all European absolutism was morally defeated and, on
the contrary, European liberalism, which was struggling and
bridling in repression, became an example of how to face the
enemy in extreme cases; a proof that in this way victory is certain;
an aid in the fact itself that a great power had reached the
plenitude of liberty; and ground for confidence in revolutions soon
to come. After fifteen years, after all the efforts of the governments,
the wiles of the police, the labours of the gendarmes and militias,

SOURCE: Benedetto Croce, *History of Europe in the Nineteenth Century,* translated by
Henry Furst, London: George Allen & Unwin, 1953, pp. 101-2, 156-9, 161-2.

absolutism, which in the intellectual field had shown its feebleness
and lack of logic, allowed itself to be beaten even in the field that
was all its own, and in which it felt itself more at ease, in that of
the force which it is customary to call material. And, in these
fifteen years, liberalism had made such great progress as to render
democracy dependent on it and to attract the better elements even
of the aristocracy and Catholicism. These combats in the streets of
Paris attained to the significance of a world-battle; it seemed to
the anxious watchers that the thick black clouds which were
lowering on the horizon of European political life had suddenly
been scattered by the sun, by the "July sun."

France. . .had raised its freely conceded constitutional charter
to a negotiated constitution, deprived the monarch of the power to
issue ordinances (which had been the incentive for the July
insurrection), transformed the hereditary chamber of peers into a
chamber nominated for life by the king, diminished the amount of
property required in order to exercise the suffrage— thereby
doubling the number of electors, which rose to two hundred
thousand and then grew to two hundred and forty thousand—
reinstituted the National Guard, suppressed the article concerning
the religion of the state, and abolished the censorship on books
and newspapers. But the life of the organism thus formed was
differently interpreted by the two parties that had brought it into
the world, which took the opposite names of Movement and
Resistance. For the men of the Movement, the establishment of the
July monarchy was a necessary but only an initial step, to be
followed promptly by others directed towards liberal reforms in
every branch of society and in an ever greater participation of the
people in the Government. It was to favour a similar movement in
all Europe, and indeed to lead it, restoring to France in this sphere
the leadership which not only would form her moral greatness, but
would give her the greatness of a power, and undo or correct, in
regard to her also, the treaties of 1815. . . .

A liberal government is treasonable to its own character and
violates the intimate law of its being if it is not a government for
the acquisition of ever greater liberty; and even the political
necessities that it has to bear in mind in its relations with the
other states, and which oblige it to respect antiliberal regimes and
even at times to ally itself with them for international ends and to

allow them a free hand in their conservative and reactionary internal politics, do not justify the absolute desertion of the defence of liberty in the world, which is the animating principle of its life, a defence that must persist even in occasional retreats, in temporary renunciations, ever ready to advance again and not only to profit by the course of events but to prepare it. Otherwise the policy of a government loses what is usually called its "line," which is, in the last resort, the line of a people's history.

The men of the July Government, on the contrary, considered liberty as a *res condita* and not perpetually *condenda*, and the established regime as one that satisfied the demands of reason by choosing the golden mean between two extremes, a mean, to tell the truth, that was not synthetic nor dialectical, that is, mobile in its movement, but analytic and static and imposing a goal on movement; it was called a *juste milieu* and became an object of disesteem and satire. This rigidity of theirs was opposed by the equally rigid abstractions of radicalism and republicanism with their persistent confidence in the facile methods of Jacobins and conventionalists, and prepared inevitable revolutionary outbursts and fearful upheavals and a dark future. It did not come, as many fancied, from a rare natural aptitude of the French people for free government, but from historical conditions and, one might say, from historical experience and at the same time from historical inexperience. During half a century France had been flung from one revolution into another, and from one dictatorship into another, from the revolution of 1789 into the Jacobin dictatorship, from Thermidor to the dictatorship of Napoleon, and then to the restoration of the monarchy with a charter of liberty, and then to the overthrow of that monarchy.

She had been waiting, but always in vain, so it proved, for this process to be closed, which was so different from her history and from that of her monarchy. These experiences, these vain hopes, induced her to cling, after so many fruitless happenings, to the regime that was established and which seemed likely to satisfy every temperate soul, and led her to look askance on innovations that might endanger it and let loose the revolutionary torrent. And inexperience or too short practice of free life had not yet permitted the formation of that sense of change and of continuity at the same time which the English people possessed, not indeed by a gift of nature, but through historical development. So that there was too much fear of conflicts, too little consciousness of the strength derived from opposition and of the utility of the alternation of parties in power, too little persuasion of the necessity to refresh, gradually, minds and spirits, and to renew the ruling political class. So these men, who were remarkable for their talent and their knowledge and their personal probity and their disinterested love of the state, rejected every demand for electoral reform that would have done away with the exclusive criterion of property. . . .

And since Louis Philippe, who had gradually, with great shrewdness and finesse, freed himself from the politicians who annoyed him or had turned them into instruments of his own, handled foreign affairs personally, this policy assumed more and more the character of action directed towards the sole end of maintaining the House of Orleans on the Throne. If a closed oligarchy, with a very restricted electoral basis, kept the Government for itself and excluded from it by far the greatest part of the French people, this very oligarchy was, in reality, overwhelmed by an extra-parliamentary power. It was in vain that parliamentary coalitions were attempted in order to remove this personal power, and in vain that Thiers concocted the doctrine that "the king reigns and does not govern"; it did not pass into French practice, whereas about the same time it was being thoroughly carried out in England. The ardour, the courage, the impetus, the faith, that had animated the liberals in the years of the restoration were gone; of the Doctrinaires, such as were not dead had grown, as it were, cold and spent, almost as though it were not possible for men to sustain in their individual life two great struggles, one after the other, and as though they has worn themselves out in the first.

20 *Dominique Bagge*

Dominique Bagge provides a modern French political scientist's verdict on the French liberals of the Restoration.

Heirs of the spirit of the eighteenth century, disillusioned witnesses of the Revolution of 1789, hesitant victims of imperial ambitions, the French individualists, fearing for their restored hopes in 1815, oriented their movement around a negative focus. The dialogue between the individual and the State became, in their estimation, a battle in which a right conceded to one party was at the same time a penalty inflicted on the other. And the struggle became the more bitter, and its thrusts the more finely calculated, the more their unanimous feeling that order was necessary forced them all, from Daunou to Guizot, to apportion generously the part to be played by authority.

In these conditions any solution required a distribution of functions. Recourse was accordingly had to the old theory of the balance of powers, in whose name the Doctrinaires, for example, for a long time did not accept the parliamentary game. The theory of popular sovereignty was rejected—or, as in the case of Constant, admitted only within stultifying limits—and, with the exception of Tracy, a careful distinction was drawn between the *individual* and his "independent" rights and the *elector* whose property qualifications were to guarantee his leisure, his intelligence, and his interests. Furthermore, although the representation of all *opinions* was rejected, that of all *interests* was supported. Equality became a dogma while inequalities were a fortunate necessity.

The *rights* of the individual were simply weapons or defenses

SOURCE: Dominique Bagge, *Les idees politiques en France sous la Restauration.* Paris: Presses Universitaires de France, 1952, pp. 159-160. [Some of the numerous italics of the original have been omitted in this translation.]

against the ruling power. *Liberties*—in the plural, except for the *republicans*— were turned into *oppositions*. . . .

Intermediary bodies were kept or reconstituted, though weakened, on the calculation that they would act as a brake on the authority of the state without reducing the independence of individuals. In this respect they were usually placed either a little outside the State-individual relationship— as in the case of the peerage—or at a reasonable distance away from power— as in the case of the local assemblies—or under formal discipline, as in the case of officials; for liberty was held to flow from accepted forms.

But, entangled in such a complicated mechanism, the notion of individual rights rapidly lost its inviolable character. Although Constant was still indefatigably proclaiming them, Mme. de Stael, a great admirer of Bentham, affirmed a link between right and utility, while Royer-Collard and Guizot sought no ground for rights beyond necessity.

It is curious to note that none of the individualist politicians claimed to adhere in the abstract to any precise form of government, perhaps because they were tired of trying to find a reality to attach to their ideal. And even though they had their preferences, and though the flexibility of the text of the Charter, moreover, offered them the possibility, which they avidly exploited, of endless fine distinctions, their concern for preserving the restored order of things took precedence over any other preoccupation.

They admired the English and American examples. But Royer-Collard rejected any transplantation on the ground that the difference in historical structures would nullify it, while Constant wished lessons to be learned. . ..

Although themselves descended from a revolutionary tradition they felt repugnance toward any revolution. But they were acutely aware of the current of social evolution running through the country and without worrying about doctrine resolutely joined in it, each of them according to his own angle of vision, his origin, his ideology. Destutt de Tracy and [Paul-Louis] Courier were already democrats, Royer-Collard and Guizot were bourgeois. Mme. de Stael and Benjamin Constant opted for an aristocracy of the intelligentsia.

Their interest in social affairs stopped short of the economic sphere. They never proclaimed the right to work, and this was the main ground on which they were reproached by such a man as

[Charles] Fourier, whose extreme individualism was at the same time a precursor of socialism. When they spoke of free trade they did so uncertainly, and when they suggested intervention in economic life they did so hesitantly.

Their embarrassment when confronted with anything positive is manifest. They were essentially *negative* men. . . . They were essentially negative men. . ..

CONCLUSION

Tocqueville's warnings to the squabbling bourgeoisie in 1848 that in tearing each other apart they would destroy liberalism were matched in prescience by his long-run premonitions of the shape of things to come. The archetype of the classical liberal, Tocqueville foresaw with remarkable accuracy that the future lay with strong men and vulgar men who would come together and crush between them the liberals, whose essential moderation depended on a climate of educated tolerance and political sophistication. If the bourgeoisie had lost faith in themselves even under the July Monarchy, the course of the Revolution of 1848 could only undermine that faith still further. The pattern was not unlike that of 1789 to 1799 but telescoped into a shorter period. A phase of moderate rule gave way to bloody uprisings and bloody suppression and then to the election of Louis Napoleon as Prince-President and ultimately to the *coup d'etat* by which he established himself as emperor and to "plebiscitarian democracy" as the form of government which allowed him at one and the same time to outflank the liberals and to secure his more or less arbitrary rule by the apparent consent of the majority.

Like his uncle Napoleon III tried, at the end of his reign, to liberalize his regime, only to be overtaken by events in the form of defeat at the hands of Bismarck's Prussia. Here again there was some poetic justice, for Bismarck had learned much of the art of overcoming internal liberal resistance from Napoleon III. In fact the decline of liberalism after 1848 was a general European phenomenon, only Britain among the major countries being relatively immune. The revolutions of 1848 were basically liberal revolutions in origin and in intent, and the liberals of Europe could not hide from themselves the fact that the failure of the revolutions meant above all the failure of liberalism to seize the best opportunity it was ever likely to have.

Yet in due course they rallied, in Europe in general and probably in France in particular. The Third Republic was governed, more or less, most of the time by politicians who could be generally described as liberal in their inclinations (if convictions is too strong a term). More recently, much of the underlying resistance to the neo-Bonapartist autocracy of General de Gaulle was liberal in character, even if his departure was immediately precipitated by other forces; and when his successor, for example, relaxed state control over broadcasting this was described, appropriately, as indicative of a "liberalization" of the regime.

But the abiding legacy of the two generations of French liberals treated in this book lies less in the activities of their successors than in the understanding not only of politics and society but of human nature that they achieved, in the truths that they uttered and to which they clung often in adversity, and above all in the variety that they not only displayed but fostered. European civilization would have been, and would still be, very much poorer without them.

A NOTE ON FURTHER READING

The literature on French history and on liberalism in the period treated is vast, and no attempt at anything even approaching a complete catalogue can be made here. A few key books on various aspects of the subject in English are listed below. For more detailed references and for works in French (far more numerous, of course) the student should consult the bibliographies of the books listed, the American Historical Association's *Guide to Historical Literature* (New York, 1961), and periodicals such as the *American Historical Review*, the *Journal of Modern History*, and *French Historical Studies*, all of which contain reviews of and references to the most recent publications as well as articles of their own.

Crane Brinton, A *Decade of Revolution, 1789-1799* (New York and London, 1934).

J. M. Thompson, *The French Revolution* (New York, 1945).

Leo Gershoy, *The French Revolution and Napoleon* (New York, 1939).

M. J. Sydenham, *The Girondins* (London, 1961).

Alfred Cobban, *A History of Modern France* (2 vols., Penguin Books, 1957/61).

Guillaume de Bertier de Sauvigny, *The Bourbon Restoration*, tr. Lynn M. Case (Philadelphia, 1966).

Guido de Ruggiero, *The History of European Liberalism*, tr. R. G. Collingwood (Boston, 1959).

Douglas Johnson, *Guizot: Aspects of French History, 1789-1874* (London and Toronto, 1963).

Vincent E. Starzinger, *Middlingness:* Juste Milieu *Political Theory in France and England, 1815-1848* (Charlottesville, Va., 1965).

.